Contents

Britain in 1700

Key Ideas
1. Britain was different in 1700 from today
2. Britain was ready to change

Core Skills
1. Comprehension
2. Vocabulary
3. Information finding
4. Transfer of information

At home

Britain in 1700 was a very different place from Britain towards the end of the twentieth century. The country earned its living from agriculture rather than from manufacture.

► What is a granary? What do you think Moll means by saying that Britain was the 'Granary of the Western World'?

SOURCE 1 — Fertile land

The soil here is so very fruitful, especially in Corn, that the Island was called the Granary of the Western World; and we think it may still deserve that name.

(Herman Moll, 'A New Description of England and Wales', 1724)

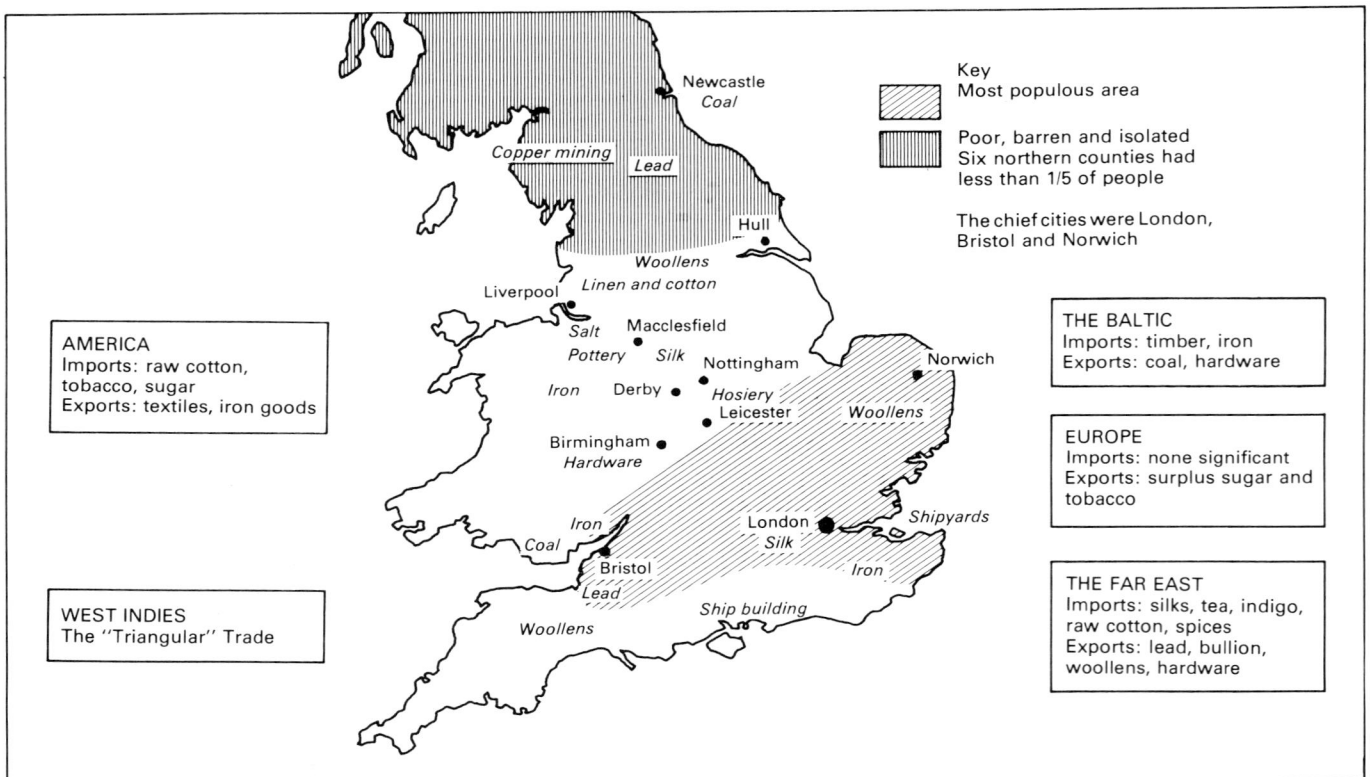

Britain in the 1700s.

► Which are the six northern counties?

► Look at cigarettes and tobacco advertisements or packets. In which cities are the tobacco companies mainly based? Can you think why?

► What is an apothecary?

Peter Gaskell, an apothecary and surgeon, writing in 1833 remembered the past:

SOURCE 2 — People worked at home

Prior to the year 1760, manufactures were in a great measure confined to the demands of the home market. At this period the majority of the artisans had laboured in their own houses.

(The Manufacturing Population of England)

4

British Social and Economic History

Industrial Change

This ... is to be returned on or before

Ian Meadowcroft

Holmes McDougall,   Edinburgh

Acknowledgements

The author and the publisher acknowledge the following illustration sources. They have made every effort to trace the copyright holders, but where they have failed they will be happy to make the necessary arrangements at the first opportunity.

Barrow-in-Furness Borough Library   **42** (bottom)
Beamish Museum   **58**
Bristol Museum and Art Gallery   **14** (bottom)
Hulton Picture Company   **11, 13, 15** (bottom), **59** (top and bottom), **82, 85, 97**
Illustrated London News Picture Library   **30,75**
Ironbridge Gorge Museum   **39, 40**
Manchester City Art Gallery   **5**
Manchester Public Libraries: Local History Library   **17** (top), **21, 22, 27, 28, 35, 45, 47, 48, 83** (top and bottom)
Mansell Collection   **6, 14** (top), **15** (top), **18, 37, 56, 57, 63, 70** (top and bottom), **77, 87, 89**
National Maritime Museum   **51, 72**
Punch   **93**
Science Museum   **17** (bottom), **42** (top), **66**
Tyne and Wear   **52, 53** (bottom), **54**
Josiah Wedgwood & Son Ltd.   **24** (top and bottom)

We wish to thank Octopus Publishing Group for permission to use extracts from *Business in Britain* by G. Turner, Basil Blackwell for permission to redraw the artwork on page 26 and Durham County Council Environment Department for permission to redraw the artwork on page 65.

Illustrations by David Wilson

Cover picture: Detail from 'Royal Visit to Sheffield: Casting Steel Ingots at Messrs. Firth and Sons' Factory' by courtesy of the Sheffield City Museum

Holmes McDougall Ltd, Allander House, 137-141 Leith Walk, Edinburgh EH6 8NS

ISBN 0 7157 2770-2

Printed and bound in Great Britain, by Holmes McDougall, Edinburgh

No man on earth had ever travelled faster than the speed of a galloping horse, while water was best to move heavy or bulky goods. To move heavy goods from Manchester to Leeds, it was best to go down the Rivers Irwell and Mersey to Liverpool, round the north of Scotland to Hull by ship, and up the Rivers Humber and Aire to Leeds.

▶ Which items of the National Income would you expect to have a higher percentage today than in 1700? Which items would you expect to have a lower percentage?

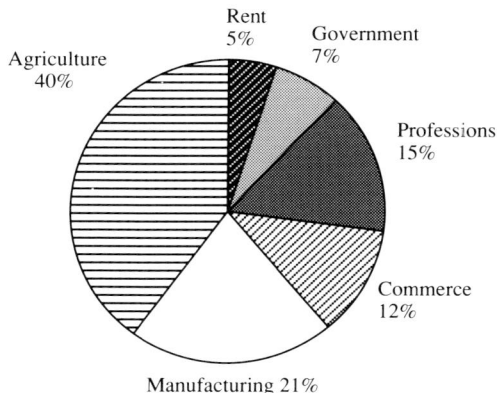

Rent 5%
Government 7%
Agriculture 40%
Professions 15%
Commerce 12%
Manufacturing 21%

There were fewer people altogether. In 1700 the population of England and Wales was only 5½ million. Towns that were then thought to be huge, like Bristol or Norwich, the two largest cities after London, had only about 25 000 people. This is about the same as Barnstaple or Newmarket today.

A country fair.

Gregory King, a Treasury official, made a survey of the British people in 1696 for the purposes of trade and taxation. He found that the ten most common jobs, from highest to lowest, were: 'Labourers and servants, Farmworkers, Craftsmen, Seamen, Shopkeepers and traders, Gentlemen, Merchants, Clergymen, Government officials, Lawyers.'

By 1700 however things were beginning to change. The population was increasing. Britain was gaining an empire. The Navigation Acts 1660 severely limited trade with British colonies by any other country but Britain. The most profitable trade of all was the 'triangular trade'. The system was simple:

► What are hardwares?

► Which part of America were the slaves usually taken to?

1. British ships took cloth, hardware, guns and rum to West Africa. These goods were then exchanged for slaves.
2. The ships then carried the slaves to North America or the West Indies, where they were exchanged for sugar, cotton and tobacco. The merchants could still make a profit if half the slaves died.
3. The sugar, cotton and tobacco were brought to Britain, mostly to Bristol or Liverpool, where they were sold. Sugar was made into rum, cotton into cloth and the whole cycle began again.

SOURCE 3 — Britain becomes rich

England produces of itself all the Necessities and Conveniences of Life. No other Nation can pretend the same. There is no need to talk at large on this, nor on the rich treasures the Earth affords us, in greater Plenty than our neighbouring Nations; such as Lead, tin, Copper, Coals, etc. . . .

(Herman Moll, 'A New Description of England and Wales', 1724)

The prosperous city of Bath in 1734.

Questions

1. On an outline map of England and Wales mark in all the places and rivers mentioned in the text, mark in the journey that heavy goods would have made from Manchester to Leeds. The goods would have had to be loaded onto different boats at Liverpool and Hull. Can you think why?

2. What are, or were:
   artisans?   clergymen?   craftsmen?

3. Can you find out what the ten most common jobs are today? You will need to get information from the census. Your local library should have a copy.

4. On an outline map of the world mark in areas that were British colonies in 1700.

5. The 'Triangular Trade' helped to make Britain rich. What do you think it did for the countries in West Africa? Explain your answer.

6. Explain why it was important for Britain to be politically stable if the country was to develop? Why would it help that it was possible to change social clases?

7. Make a list of things you would see in a picture of a major town today that you do not see in the picture of Bath in 1734.

8. Design an advertisement, or a brochure, for a holiday in the England of 1700.

Population

A growing problem

The slow growth in population that had been going on since the Norman Conquest changes to a 'population explosion' in the eighteenth century which has been going on ever since.

Changes in the population of England and Wales.

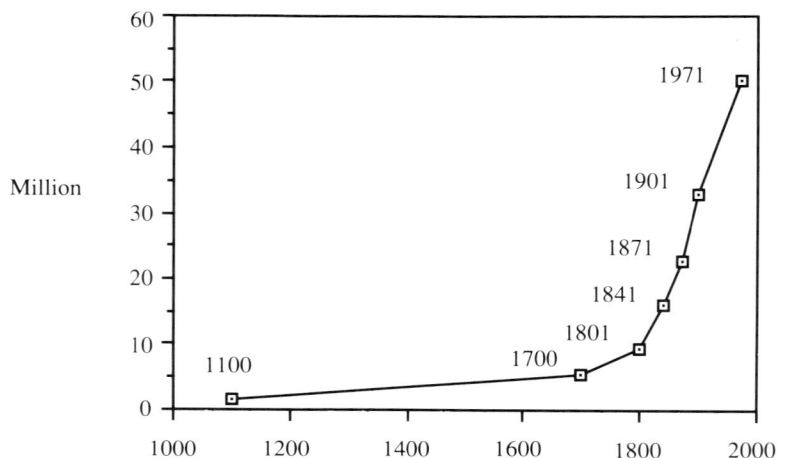

► What, approximately, would the population of England and Wales have been in 1500?

► The population of England and Wales has clearly been growing much quicker since about 1700. Can you find any reasons why this might be so? You might consider food, clothes and medicine. Can you think of anything else?

There are only four possible ways that the population can change. This is due to change in the:

a.   birth rate
b.   death rate
c.   immigration rate
d.   emigration rate

The birth rate is the number of births per thousand of the population. It is found by counting the number of births and dividing them by the number of thousands of people there are in the country. The death rate is the number of deaths per thousand of the population. The natural rate of increase (or decrease) is found by taking away the death rate from the birth rate.

If these calculations are to be done it is necessary to count the number of births, deaths, people, etc. accurately. Gregory King made a survey of the population in 1695 (see Britain in 1700), but regular counting did not begin until 1801. Since 1801 there has been a census, to count the population, every ten years (except 1941 during World War II). The first censuses asked only a few simple questions so the information gained was rather limited but from 1841 we have a much fuller picture. Before the census became really effective we have to make estimates based on records kept by churches, tax records etc. which are not always very accurate.

▶ Thomas Malthus thought that population could never grow very large as there would not be enough food. In what ways would a shortage of food help to keep down the population?

▶ Malthus would have been astonished to see the way the population has risen over the last 200 years. Can you explain in what way his theory was wrong?

▶ Between what years was there a 'natural decrease' in the population?

▶ Britain does not grow enough food to feed its people today. Why does the famine that Malthus promised not come and reduce the population?

▶ Where did most people live in 1801? How had this changed by 1901?

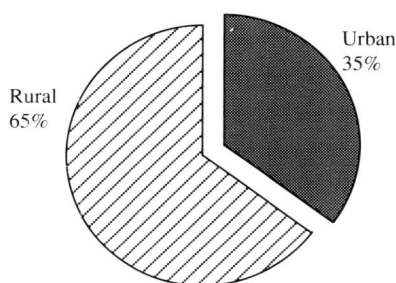

SOURCE 4 — Population growth
1. Population is limited by the quantity of food available.
2. Population increases where the quantity of food increases, unless prevented by powerful checks.
3. These checks are all resolvable into moral restraint, vice and misery.

(T.R. Malthus, 'An Essay on the Principle of Population', 1803)

In the eighteenth century movement of population was probably not a significant factor. Immigrants did come to England and Wales but thousands went to the colonies. In the nineteenth century however the picture changed. During the middle years of the century over six million people emigrated overseas. There was immigration too but it was probably not a significant factor in population growth at this time.

Rural 65% Urban 35%

Percentage of the population living in towns, 1801

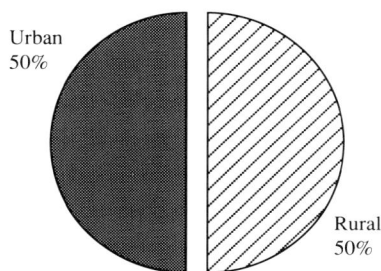

Urban 50% Rural 50%

Percentage of the population living in towns, 1851

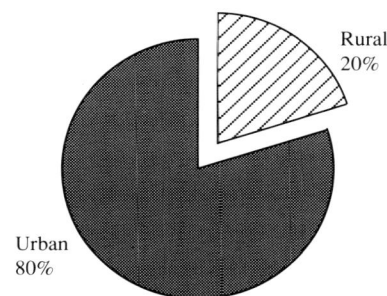

Rural 20% Urban 80%

Percentage of the population living in towns, 1901

Changes of population in rural and urban areas.

Life in the country: "Hengar House" by the artist Rowlandson.

The proof

SOURCE 5 — Birth and death rates in England and Wales

Date	Births*	Deaths*
1700	33.1	26.0
1710	27.5	26.7
1720	30.5	29.7
1730	32.0	32.0
1740	33.3	31.7
1750	34.7	28.2
1760	33.3	26.7
1770	34.0	27.9
1780	34.4	28.8
1790	35.44	25.65
1800	34.23	23.14
1810	33.84	19.98
1820	33.39	20.33
1830	32.38	21.65
1840	31.43	20.8

*per thousand of the population

► Has the population grown mainly from more births, or from fewer deaths?

Life in the town: "Beer Street" by Hogarth.

Questions

1. The heads and tails of the following statements have been mixed. Write them out correctly.
   - (a) A census
   - (b) The birth rate
   - (c) An immigrant
   - (d) An emigrant
   - (e) Natural Increase
   - i. comes from abroad to live here.
   - ii. comes when birth rate is higher than death rate.
   - iii. measures the number of births per thousand of the population.
   - iv. is a count of the population.
   - v. goes to live abroad.
2. What, exactly, is meant by the term death rate?
3. Draw line graphs of the birth rate and death rate on the same axes. Label your graph clearly. Shade in the area showing the natural increase of the population. Between which years was there a natural decrease in the population?
4. In what way does 'Beer Street' show how the growth in population was affecting the towns?
5. Research has shown that richer families tended to have fewer children than poorer families (certainly until recently), yet they can afford to have more. Can you think of any explanations why this might be so.
   (Hint: Consider the problem of earning a living.)

Early Industry

Key Ideas
1. Britain was still largely agricultural
2. The whole family worked
3. Work was done mostly at or from home
4. There were some large scale industry
5. Problems of transport

Core Skills
1. Investigation
2. Use of evidence

Domestic system

During the early years of the eighteenth century most people worked at their own home, or on the land round it.

▶ What is meant by 'raised their rents'?

SOURCE 6 — Life in Mellor, near Stockport
. . . the land was occupied by between 50 and 60 farmers, and out of these farmers there were only 6 or 7 who raised their rents directly from the produce of their farms. All the rest got their rent partly in some branch of trade such as spinning and weaving woollen, linen or cotton (cloth). The cottagers were employed entirely in this manner except for a few weeks in the harvest.
(William Radcliffe, 1770)

SOURCE 7 — Life in Birmingham
In the country round about are nailers and woodscrew makers, who work in their own cottages. The women and children, as well as the men are employed in the manufacture of these articles. Sometimes the whole family will be occupied in one branch of business, the father of the family makes large nails, and the wife and children smaller ones according to their strength.
(William Thompson, 'Tour of England and Scotland', 1788)

The pattern was the same throughout most trades of the British Isles. The family worked together at the family trade. Everybody was involved from the youngest to the oldest.

▶ What is a 'tenter'?

SOURCE 8 — The manufacture of woollen cloth, West Riding
We could see at every house a tenter, and on almost every tenter a piece of cloth. (At every one of them) we found a gutter of running water. The dyeing houses, scouring-shops and (other) places emitted the water again tinged with the drugs of the dyeing fat, and with the oil, and soap, the tallow, and other ingredients used by the clothiers.

Every clothier must keep a horse to fetch and carry for the use of his manufacture, to fetch home his wool, to carry his yarn to the spinners, his cloth to the fulling mill, and then to the market to be sold. Every one keeps a cow or two for his family, and this employs the pieces of enclosed land about his house, for they scarce grow corn enough for their cocks and hens.

Amongst the clothiers houses are scattered cottages in which dwell the workmen, the women and children of whom are always busy carding, spinning etc. All employed from the youngest to the oldest; hardly anything above four years old but its hands are sufficient (to support it).
(Daniel Defoe, 'A Tour Through the Whole Island of Great Britain', 1724)

The textile regions of England.

► Which regions were particularly important for making woollen cloth?

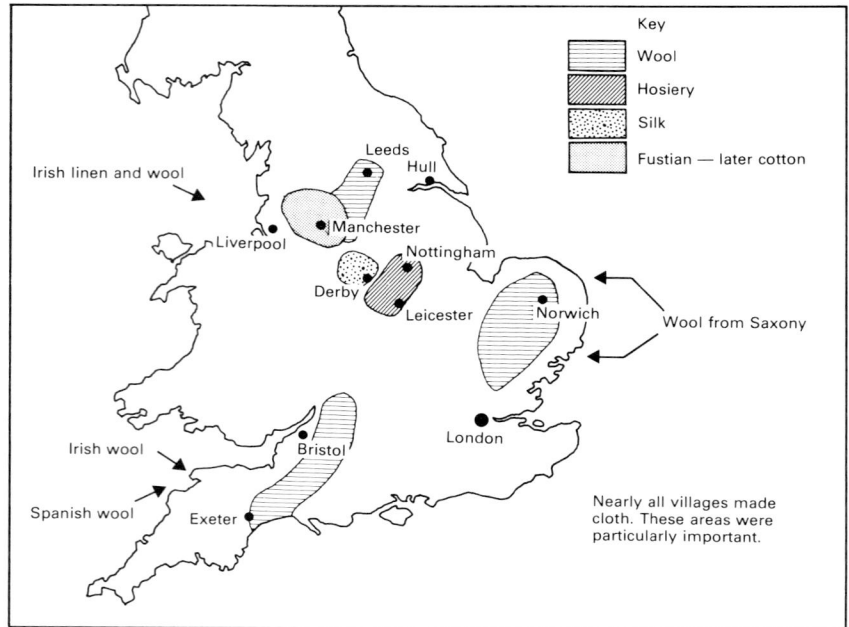

Key
Wool
Hosiery
Silk
Fustian — later cotton

Irish linen and wool
Leeds
Hull
Liverpool
Manchester
Nottingham
Derby
Leicester
Norwich
Wool from Saxony
Irish wool
Bristol
London
Spanish wool
Exeter

Nearly all villages made cloth. These areas were particularly important.

► From what is linen cloth made?

There were problems:

1. There were many disagreements between clothiers and workers. Clothiers sometimes used false weights in weighing out the cloth. On the other hand a lot of pilfering took place.
2. Pay was often low. Hours of work could be very long, and conditions bad. Cottages were often small, cold, damp, uncomfortable and polluted.
3. Work was irregular and people were laid off in slack times. Outside the West Riding workers did not usually own land to farm in spare time.
4. Young children had to work.
5. Some workers lived a long way from the clothier's, or merchant's house. A great deal of time was wasted in travelling.

Not all trades could be carried out in the home. Mining was one. Lead, tin, copper, iron and coal were all mined. Coal was used mainly in the home up to this time. The two early types of mine were the 'bellpit', and the drift mine, also known as an adit. Where possible heavy goods were carried by water. Where it was not possible they did the best they could.

SOURCE 9 — Transporting coal

. . . where the boats unload the coal, the packhorses come and take it in sacks, and so carry it to places all about. The horses carry two bushel at a time, which at the place of disembarkation cost eighteen pence, and when its brought to Taunton cost two shillings. The roads were full of these carriers going and returning.
(Celia Fiennes, 'Through England on a Side-Saddle, the Diary of Celia Fiennes', 1697)

► What weight is two bushels?

► Convert the money written about by Celia Fiennes into modern money.

It was expensive. The price of coal went up by 6d in the three miles to Taunton. It is difficult to sort out wages for Britain in 1700. They were higher in the north than the south and higher in the town than the country. A labourer in the Shropshire iron industry earned about 8s or 9s a week. Coal must have been too expensive in Devon for ordinary people.

Even in mining everything was done on a small scale. Perhaps the only industry to work on a large scale was shipbuilding on the south coast.

Different parts of the country tended to specialise in different products. East Anglia made woollen cloth, Wolverhampton made locks.

Making shoelaces, work which could be done at home.

SOURCE 10 — A family lock-making business carried out at home, 1842

Having made your way through the passage, you find yourself in a space varying in size with the number of houses it contains. These are the dwellings and workshops of the poorest of the working classes.

Locks are made by forging, pressing and filing. Children are placed standing upon blocks so as to be able to reach the vise, and set to work with a file almost as soon as they can hold one.
(R.H. Horne, 'Childrens' Employment Commission', 1842)

SOURCE 11 — Glass-making in Bristol

The great demand for glass bottles for the use of Town and Country keep the various bottle glasshouses here constantly at work. The call for window glass at home, at Bath and in the Towns about Bristol: in the Western Counties, Wales and from North to South wherever Bristol trade extends, and the great quantities sent to America, employed several houses for this article.
('Matthew's New History of Bristol or Complete Guide and Bristol Directory for the Year 1793-4')

Questions

1. Why was this system of industry often called the 'Domestic System'? (Clue: A dictionary might help.)
2. The text talks about the difficulties with the Domestic System. Can you think of any advantages it might have?
3. There are four main processes to making cloth; carding, spinning, weaving and finishing. Find out what is meant by each. Explain and make diagrams or drawings. You might like to work as a group for this one.
4. Explain why shipbuilding was not a 'domestic' industry.
5. What indications are to be found in the sources that industry in Britain was busy and prosperous in 1700?
6. Why would the Domestic System be no good for us today?
7. What do you see as the main similarities and differences between industry in the Britain of 1700 and the Britain of today?

The Beginnings of Change

Key Ideas
1. The importance of the colonies
2. Incentive for change
3. Means available
4. The importance of social factors

Core Skills
1. Research
2. Mapwork
3. Language
4. Asking historical questions

Causes of change

Taking cloth to market.

Britain in 1700 was rich. Herman Moll said 'England produces . . . all the Necessities . . . of Life. No other Nation can pretend the same' (See 'Britain in 1700'). This was partly due to the colonies. From 1600 to 1900 the British empire grew as more colonies were gained, by one means or another. The Navigation Act 1660 made it difficult for any country except Britain to trade with British colonies. This began to make Britain rich. The colonies needed manufactured goods, which were supplied from Britain. Britain needed raw materials of all kinds, which were supplied by the colonies. The 'Triangular Trade' is only one example of this. The merchants and great companies involved became rich. There was money available to invest, and there was a greater demand for British goods overseas than Britain could cope with.

The population was increasing more rapidly. The extra mouths had to be fed, which led to changes in agriculture. It also led to a greater demand still for manufactured goods. At the same time the greater numbers of people provided workers to make these goods.

Bristol became an important trading port.

► What do we mean by the phrase 'natural resources'?

► Make a list of Britain's natural resources.

► Which of the following countries are well situated for world trade?—Britain, Greece, Italy, Switzerland, Turkey.

Britain was rich in natural resources. The damp climate helped when water power was used, and indeed is itself necessary for the manufacture of cotton cloth. This combined with the demand for goods, and the availability of money encouraged new ways of producing goods more quickly, or cheaper. At about the same time, and for similar reasons transport too began to improve. This encouraged still more change. Geographically Britain was well situated for world trade while many rivers made internal communication easy.

There were other factors also. The country was peaceful. There was no civil war in Britain after 1745, and even that had left most of Britain untouched. While Britain was involved in wars abroad she was never invaded herself. This meant that the merchants and manufacturers at home could concentrate on their businesses, while wars fought overseas encouraged the development of industries such as iron and shipbuilding.

A sign of things to come — Lombe's silk mill at Derby.

In some countries people could not move to live where they liked. This was not true in Britain. People could move to live where the work was. In some countries it was not possible to move from one social class to another, no matter how much money you made. This was not the case in Britain either. It was possible to change your class, and this encouraged people to make money, by trade and industry.

Religion too played a part. During the seventeenth and eighteenth centuries there grew up several new 'branches' of the Christian church. These were known as dissenters, or non-conformists. They encouraged hard work, thrift and sobriety. These all helped in developing trade and industry in Britain, especially as these ideas appealed to the middle class who often ran businesses. The ordinary people who joined these denominations made good workers. The Scottish education system was better than the English and many Scots, often dissenters themselves, came to England to find work.

YORK Four Days Stage-Coach.

Begins on Friday the 12th of April. 1706.

ALL that are desirous to pass from *London* to *York*, or from *York* to *London*, or any other Place on that Road, Let them Repair to the *Black Swan* in *Holbourn* in *London*, and to the *Black Swan* in *Coney street* in *York*.

At both which Places, they may be received in a Stage Coach every Monday, Wednesday and Friday, which performs the whole Journey in Four Days, (if God permits,) And sets forth at Five in the Morning.

And returns from *York* to *Stamford* in two days, and from *Stamford* by *Huntington* to *London* in two days more. And the like Stages on their return.

Allowing each Passenger 14l. weight, and all above 3d a Pound.

Performed By { Benjamin Kingman, Henry Harrison, Walter Baynes.

Also this gives Notice that Newcastle Stage Coach, sets out from York, every Monday, and Friday, and from Newcastle every Monday and Friday.

An advertisement for a coach service between London and York, 1706.

The economic system began to change to cope with the changing commercial and industrial situation. Banks began to develop. The Bank of England had been founded in 1694 but probably more useful for manufacturers was the growth of local banks during the early years of the eighteenth century. These banks were all independent, not like the banks of today which have lots of branches in different places. The Stock Exchange (where men bought and sold shares in companies) developed, originally at Jonathan's Coffee House in Change Alley.

It is not easy to pick out a single factor that triggered off the industrial changes. Some people have claimed it was the growth of population, others have said it was foreign trade, or the social system. All these however were changing fairly slowly, while the changes in industry came fairly quickly. Perhaps it was just the way all the factors came together at one time. Whatever the trigger was, changes in industry were to come so fast, and were so great that it is referred to as a revolution, the 'Industrial Revolution'.

Questions

1. The words and the definitions in the following lists are mixed up. Match up each word with the correct definition.
   WORDS
   a. invest
   b. dissenters (or non-conformists)
   c. thrifty
   d. sober
   e. denomination
   f. economic
   g. commercial
   h. incentive

   DEFINITIONS
   1. to do with money or wealth
   2. careful with money
   3. an encouragement to do something
   4. to lend, to use, money hoping to make a profit
   5. to do with trade, buying and selling
   6. not reckless, not drunk
   7. sect, or branch, of the Christian church eg Catholic, Church of England
   8. branches of the Christian church which grew up in the seventeenth and eighteenth centuries, which encouraged hard work

2. Among the manufacturing towns that grew up were Birmingham, Leeds, Manchester and Nottingham. Mark these on an outline map of England and Wales. Mark in and name the rivers that would be used to take their goods to the sea.
   Mark in and name the ports that served these towns and the areas round them.

3. On the same map mark in different colours where natural resources are to be found in Britain. Mark in London. Give your map a title. Do not forget a key.

4. Make a list of denominations that were founded between 1650 and 1850.

5. The Stock Exchange grew out of a coffee house. Write a paragraph about coffee houses. Lloyds started in a coffee house too. What is Lloyds famous for? How might Lloyds have helped in the changes in industry?

6. Mark in, on an outline map of the world, the British Empire in 1700. If you can, mark in, in a different colour, the places that Britain traded with that were not colonies.
   N.B. Countries that are part of the empire are called colonies.

7. Make a list of the causes of the Industrial Revolution. Divide it up into groups, geographical, due to government action, and due to individuals. Is there any other group of causes you would like to include?

8. If you were asked to write an essay on the causes of the Industrial Revolution, what else would you try to find out to add to what you are told above?

The Coming of the Factory

Key Ideas
1. Inventions come in response to a need
2. The changing balance between spinners and weavers
3. The Water Frame meant factories
4. The position of entrepreneurs

Core Skills
1. Empathy
2. Language

New inventions

Quarry Bank Mill.

▶ What caused the changes in cotton manufacture?
▶ What caused people to try to improve spinning?

The growing population and the increasing wealth of the country meant that there was a growing demand for goods of many kinds. This included cloth and it was in the textile trade that the changes really began.

SOURCE 12 — Growth in the textile trade
. . . large exports for foreign trade and the interior business of the country is such that no exertion by workmen could have answered the demands without the introduction of spinning machines. People saw children from nine to twelve years of age manage these machines with dexterity and bring plenty into families that were before overburdened with children.
(James Ogden, 'A Description of Manchester', 1783)

In 1733 John Kay of Bury invented the Flying Shuttle. Under this system the shuttle was 'thrown' across the loom at high speed. There were two results:
a. Weaving was much faster,
b. Broader cloth could now be made.
It was the former that was so important. Weaving was now so quick that the spinners could not keep up.

There were many attempts to improve the spinning process without success, but in 1767 the Spinning Jenny was built by James Hargreaves of Blackburn. The 'Jenny' spun eleven spindles at once. It was small and worked by hand, under the Domestic System. Although spinning was much faster there were still problems. It spun a fine yarn that was suitable for the weft threads but not for the warp. People were looking for something better.

James Hargreave's Spinning Jenny.

Richard Arkwright, inventor of the Water Frame.

▶ What idea did Arkwright get from the silk industry?

▶ What is meant by 'op cit.'?

Results

▶ What effect do you think the invention of the spinning machines had on the earnings of spinners?

Number of watermills in England in 1797.

SOURCE 13 — Spinning

The majority of artisans laboured in their own homes, and in the bosoms of their families . . . and the various mechanical contrivances were expressly framed for this purpose. The distaff, the spinning wheel, producing a single thread, and, subsequently the jenny, were to be found forming part of the household furniture in almost every house.
(R. Gaskell, 'The Manufacturing Population of England', 1833)

One answer came from a Preston barber and wigmaker called Richard Arkwright. In 1769 he produced a Water Frame which produced a strong yarn suitable for the warp threads. It was however rather coarse and many weavers used 'Jenny' thread for the weft and 'Water Frame' thread for the warp. Arkwright may have stolen the idea for his machine from another inventor but there is no doubt that he was a brilliant entrepreneur and developed the factory system as we know it.

SOURCE 14 — The rise of entrepreneurs

The men who did establish themselves were raised by their own efforts—commencing in a very humble way, having a very limited capital, or even none at all save their own labour . . . the celerity with which some of these individuals accumulated great wealth are proofs that they were men of quick views, great energy of character, and possessing no small share of sagacity.
(Gaskell, op. cit.)

SOURCE 15 — Factories

The modern miracles, my friend, are to me the machines here and the buildings that house them, called factories.
(Christian P.W. Beuth, 'Letter to K.F. Schinkel', 1823)

Life in the textile trades was never the same again. Spinners first and later weavers worked not at home but in the 'manufactory'. Machines were driven by power not by hand. They increased in size and jennies too became worked by water power. At the time of Hargreaves' death there were jennies fitted with 80 spindles. People had to work when the factory was working, not when they chose. If scores of people were to work together in a factory they had to stick to rules, whether they liked them or not. Factories were built where there were fast flowing streams to drive the wheels, and people had to live where the factories were.

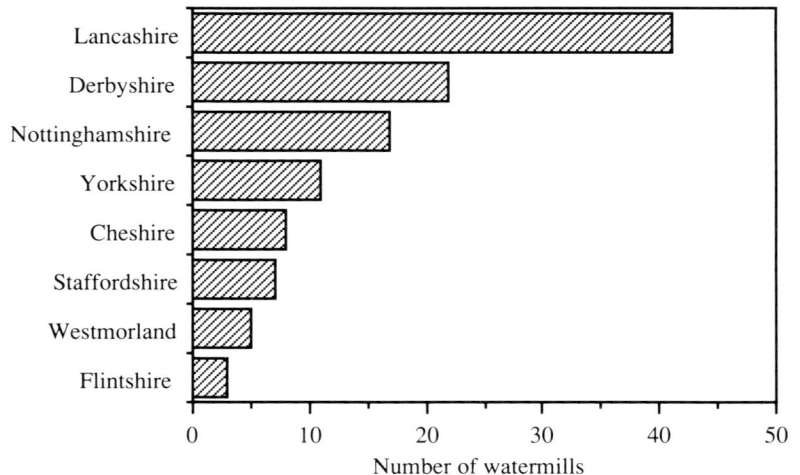

Number of watermills

Lancashire, Derbyshire, Nottinghamshire, Yorkshire, Cheshire, Staffordshire, Westmorland, Flintshire

0 10 20 30 40 50

Machines in 1811

(bar chart showing machines in millions: Jenny ~0.2, Frame ~0.3, Mule ~4.2)

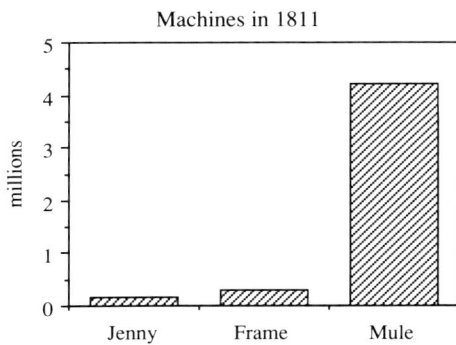

If Arkwright's Water Frame was successful there was a still more successful machine to come. This was the 'Mule' invented by Samuel Crompton in 1779. It was so called because, like the mule it was a cross, in this case between the Spinning Jenny and the Water Frame. The thread was very strong and very fine. It was exactly what the cotton trade needed. Although Mules had been worked by hand and continued to be so as late as the 1870s for the very finest counts, it was not really a machine for domestic industry. It was large, expensive and demanded a great deal of power to drive it. By 1825 Roberts had fitted Mules with 2000 spindles. It was a machine for the new factories, and it made a fortune for the factory masters who used it.

SOURCE 16 — Cotton
Now cotton yarn is cheaper than linen yarn, and cotton goods are very much used in place of cambric, lawns, and other expensive fabrics of flax, and they have almost totally superseded the silks. Women of all ranks, from the highest to the lowest, are clothed in British manufactures of cotton.
('Macpherson Annals of Commerce', 1805)

SOURCE 17
The manufactures called Manchester wares, such as fustians, cottons, tapes, incle, &c. are sent on pack-horses to London, Bristol, Liverpool, &c. for exportation, and also to the wholesale haberdashers for home consumption. Of these goods they make, at Manchester, Bolton, and the neighbouring places, above £600,000 annually.
(Postlethwayt, 'Universal Dictionary of Trade and Commerce', 1766)

SOURCE 18 — The impact of the weavers
The mule twist, with an increasing demand for every fabric the loom could produce, put all hands in request. The price of labour rose to five times the amount ever experienced in this district, every family bringing home weekly 40, 60, 80, 100, or even 120 shillings per week!
(William Radcliffe, 'Origin of the New System of Manufacture', 1828)

▶ Although the Spinning Jenny and the Water Frame were both competing with each other to produce cotton cloth, they both did well in the late eighteenth century. Explain why this was.

▶ What is meant by 'mule twist'?
▶ What are
   distaffs?   incles (or inckles)?
   haberdashers?   fustians?
   celerity?   entrepreneurs?
▶ Explain how it was that at this time weavers used to go round with £5 notes in their hatbands to show how rich they were.

Questions

1. You have gone to work in one of the new cotton factories in 1780. Explain to your son why it was better when you were a boy and worked at home. (You might consider friends, rules, foremen, pay, working conditions, hours, as a start.)
2. You are the son of the man in question 1. Explain to your father why he is better off working in a factory than under the Domestic System. (You might consider the same points as in question 1.)
3. The date is 1778. You are a cotton spinner. You have seen Arkwright's mill at Cromford and have a wish to set up such a mill yourself. You will need to borrow money. Write a letter to your brother to persuade him to lend you the cash. You will need to give as much detail about your plans as possible—what sort of place you need to build in, what type of machines you should use, why you should build a factory at all etc.
4. You are a weaver talking to your friends in the pub. In not more than ten sentences explain what you think of the changes in spinning.
5. Between 1700 and 1800 the wages of unskilled workers in London rose from 20d to 24d per day. In the same period in Lancashire they rose from 8d to 25d per day. Comment.

Early Factories 1

Key Ideas
1. Location of industry
2. The transmission of power
3. The problem of attracting workers
4. Working conditions

Core Skills
1. Use of evidence
2. Synthesis
3. Historical ideas

Location

A number of early textile factories have been preserved. They were known as mills for the only people who knew about waterwheels at this time were corn millers. As they moved from corn to cotton they took the name with them. Textile factories became 'mills'. If you visit these early mills you will find them in pleasant country surroundings, not in the factory towns that you might expect. The reason is that water powered mills were located on fast flowing streams. They had to be strung out along the streams or there was no power. There was great competition for water, which was used and re-used by many mills during the course of a stream or river.

The race for water power.

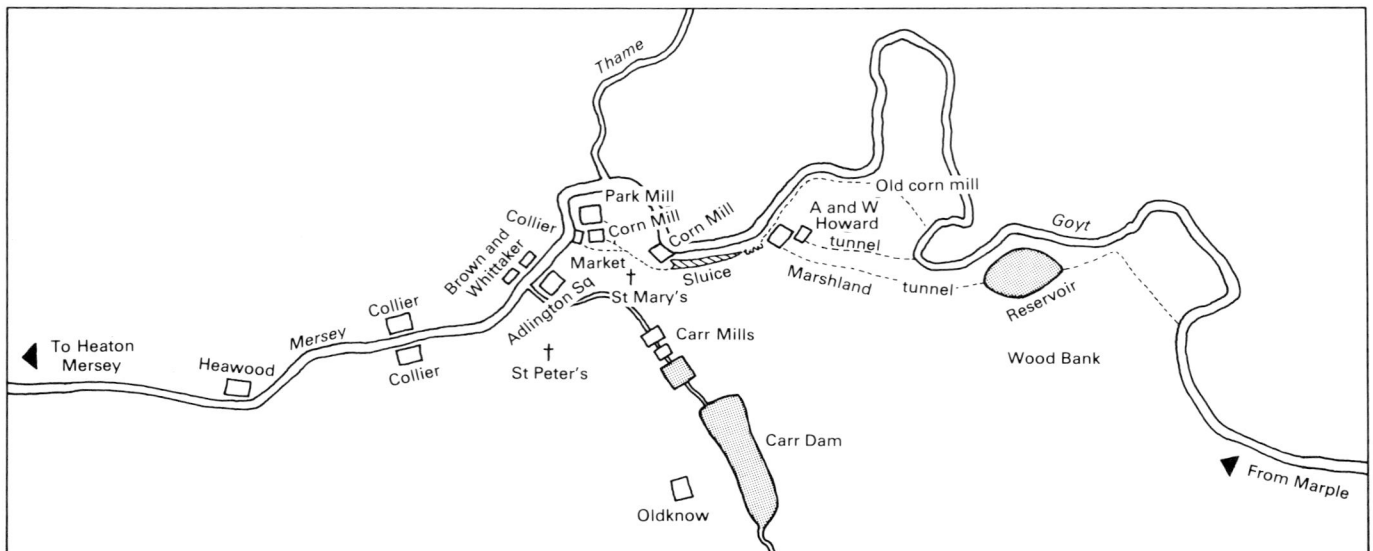

Growth

SOURCE 19 — Mills in Lanark
In the year 1784 the late Mr. Dale of Glasgow, founded a manufactory for spinning of cotton, near the falls of the Clyde, in the county of Lanark, in Scotland.

It was the power which could be obtained from the falls of water that induced Mr. Dale to erect his mills in this situation; for in other respects it was not well chosen. The country around was uncultivated; the inhabitants were poor and few in number; and the roads in the neighbourhood were bad.
(Robert Owen, 'A New View of Society', 1831)

▶ Why did it matter that
   i. the country around was uncultivated?
   ii. the inhabitants were poor and few in number?
   iii. the roads were bad?

▶ Why do you think Mr Dale founded his manufactory in 1784?

The Manchester Mercury in the late 1770s advertised many mills on streams with good sites for water wheels, at which carding and twisting machinery could be installed at little expense.

Power

Imports of raw cotton

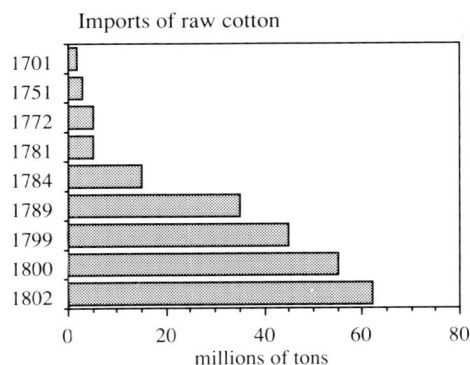

Year	millions of tons
1701	
1751	
1772	
1781	
1784	
1789	
1799	
1800	
1802	

Large factories meant large waterwheels. This wheel is ''Big Lily'' at Compstal Mill, Stockport.

Problems for workers

In 1760 only 8 000 tons of raw cotton were imported; by 1800 the figure had risen to 25 000 tons.

SOURCE 20 — Arkwright's Water Frame
It was about the year 1784 that the expiration of Sir Richard Arkwright's patent caused the erection of water machines for the spinning of warps in all parts of the country.
(Sir F.M. Eden, 'The State of the Poor', 1797)

The cotton industry was booming and many mills were built. There was great competition for water.

The new factories were built round the waterwheel. The power then had to be transmitted to each of the machines through a system of shafts which ran up the wall and along the ceiling of the rooms. From these shafts each machine had a belt which drove it, rather as the back wheel of a bicycle is driven by the pedals. It was highly successful, but it was also dangerous as there were no guards on the moving parts. It was not unusual to get an arm crushed in the belt drive.

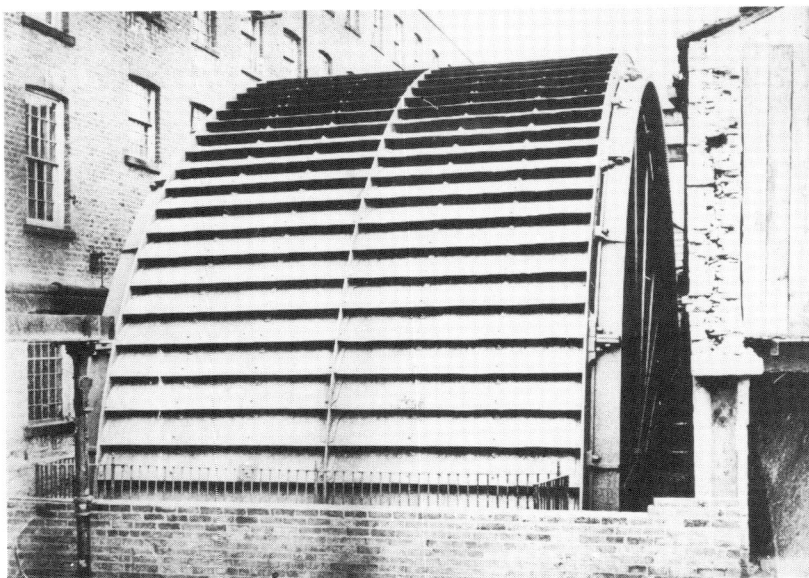

Conditions in factories varied but danger from machines was not the only problem. Usually women and children were employed rather than men. Their wages were less and, with a water wheel to provide the power, physical strength was not needed. Hours were long, twelve hours a day was usual, and in busy times fourteen hours a day and more were worked. Conditions were often bad. Temperature in a spinning mill was kept high and the atmosphere had to be humid or the cotton snapped and would not spin properly. This hot, damp atmosphere was usually thick with dust and fluff from the cotton fibres. It is hardly surprising that many workers suffered from diseases of the lungs. Long hours bent over machines and inadequate breaks did not help. Children had to bend under the machines while they were working, and had to clean the machines during their already short meal breaks. Deformities and injuries were common. Masters were often cruel—workers were beaten and forced to pay fines if they were late or made a mistake.

Spinners using Mules to spin thread.

Problems for masters

Ordinary mill hands usually came from the district round about, simply going to the mill to ask for a job. However mills were built where the water was and, as in the case of Mr. Dale of Lanark, there were few people round about. Mr. Dale decided to bring in children and to build somewhere for them to live. That was cheap, if a bit of a nuisance, but others made the same decision.

Skilled hands such as clerks, overlookers and mechanics had to be advertised for.

SOURCE 21 — An advertisement in the 'Manchester Mercury', late 1770s
a manager 'For a small Factory in the Country'
a man that 'understands Spinning and the care of Spinning Jennies'
clock-makers especially those who had been previously employed in 'Cotton Works'

SOURCE 22 — Wanted
A MAN of good Character, as an Overlooker of a Room in a Cotton-Mill, that is perfectly Master of Carding and Preparing—any one well-versed in the aforesaid Art, will meet with Encouragement by applying to the Printer of this Paper.
(*Derby Mercury*, 15th May 1794)

There were however other types of probelms too. Many people feared the coming of machines lest it bring unemployment. Hargreaves' house was broken into by the 'ignorant and misguided multitude' who destroyed his machine and part of his furniture. Hargreaves moved to Nottingham in disgust.

▶ What were overlookers? Man. (Manr.)? piece goods? shafts?

SOURCE 23 — The destruction of a mill
Mr Grimshaw of Gorton attempted the construction of machinery to weave piece goods, in a capital factory at Knott-mill, which was burnt down before any judgement could be formed how it would have succeeded.
(Sir F.M. Eden, 'The State of the Poor', 1797)

SOURCE 24 — A letter to Mr Arkwright
Sir,   Man. 28th Nov. 1782.
I am very sorry to hear that you still do all you can to distress the trade of Manr . . . I am delighted to lay in wait for you either in this town, or Nottingham, or wherever I most likely to find you. I will ashure shute you as your name is what it is dam you do you think the town must be ruled by such a Barber as you.
(*Manchester Mercury*, 31st December 1782)

▶ How much is one hundred guineas in modern money?

▶ Write out the letter to Mr Arkwright in modern English.

Mr Arkwright offered a reward of 'ONE HUNDRED GUINEAS' for information about the writer.

Changes

There were more changes coming:

SOURCE 25 — A steam-powered mill proposed
An enterprising gentleman, named Buckley, formed, in 1793, the design of erecting a factory here (Bradford) to be wrought of a steam-engine. The respectable residents of that quarter of the town threatened Mr. Buckley with an action at law should he persist. This proceeding had the desired effect, as Mr. Buckley gave up his project.
(John James, 'The History of Bradford and its Parish', 1866)

▶ Why do you think the imports of raw cotton increased so greatly in the 1780s?

The first steam-powered mill was started at Papplewick in Nottinghamshire as early as 1785.

Questions

1. What do you think were the main dangers to be found in a cotton mill of the late 1780s?
2. Do you think the workers were right to fear the new machines that were being introduced?
3. Find out all you can about Luddites. What did they try to do? What happened to them?
4. The situation of the late eighteenth century is mirrored in the late 1980s. Newspaper printers opposed the introduction of new machines. Management used the new machines anyway and many printers lost their jobs. Would the workers have been better to accept the new machines to save their jobs? Would it have been better to have retained the old machines if it meant more people having jobs?
5. The Concise Oxford Dictionary defines progress as 'forward or onward movement'. It defines change as 'alteration; the substitution of one for another'. Do you think the substitution of the factory system for the Domestic System was progress or was it merely change?
6. In what way had the life of the textile workers changed since 1700? Was anything still the same?

Early Factories 2

Key Ideas
1. Location of industry
2. Some processes were still carried out by hand
3. Division of labour
4. Marketing

Core Skills
1. Mapwork
2. Transfer of information
3. Synthesis
4. Research

Wedgwood

A Wedgwood portrait medallion of Sir Josiah Wedgwood.

▶ In what year was the Etruria works built?

Factories were now being powered by water, work was being done by machines but there was still another aspect of the factory system to be developed. This was done by Josiah Wedgwood. In 1759 he set up his own business to produce pottery near Burslem, in the district near Stoke-on-Trent known as 'The Potteries', where there had been a domestic pottery industry for centuries.

Ten years later he built Etruria works, again near Burslem.

SOURCE 26 — Etruria
I had the pleasure of viewing the Staffordshire potteries at Burslem, and the neighbouring villages which have of late been carried on with such amazing success. It dates its demand from Mr. Wedgwood (the principal manufacturer) introducing, about four years ago, the cream coloured ware, and since then the increase has been very rapid. Common clay of the county is used for the ordinary sorts; the finer kinds are made of clay from Devonshire and Dorsetshire but the flints from the Thames are all brought rough by sea, either to Liverpool or Hull.
(Arthur Young, 'A Six Months Tour through the North of England', 1770)

'Ball clay' from Devon and Dorset was used from about 1720.

Etruria factory, with the Trent and Mersey Canal in the foreground.

Division of labour

Pottery was still produced by hand, yet Wedgwood's idea was to produce it in a factory rather than in people's homes. His idea was a simple one. He divided up the traditional skills of the potter and let each worker concentrate on one skill only. Thus some workers mixed the clay, some shaped it, some fired, some decorated and some glazed. This 'division of labour' greatly increased the output per man, and it was this which made the factory system worthwhile in an industry that was still producing by hand. The idea was used in other industries too.

SOURCE 27 — Division of labour

. . . the way in which this business is now carried on, it is divided into a number of branches, one man draws out the wire; another straights it; a third cuts it; a fourth points it; a fifth grinds it at the top for receiving the head; to make the head requires two or three distinct operations; to put it on is a peculiar business; to whiten the pin is another; it is even a trade by itself to put them into the paper; and the important business of making a pin is in this manner divided into about eighteen distinct operations, which, in some manufactories, are all performed by distinct hands.
(Adam Smith, 'The Wealth of Nations', 1776)

▶ What do you understand by the phrase 'division of labour'? You might find it easier to explain with the help of a diagram.

Quality

Wedgwood was concerned with every aspect of his work. Goods which were not up to his high standard were smashed. He constantly experimented to improve his product, developing new glazes where he felt the existing ones were inadequate. He used talented artists to decorate his wares, and used pictures of famous events as a means of selling them. He was quick to spot new ideas which could be used and was an early customer for the steam engine, using it to grind the flint. Where there was no existing piece of technology he invented one, eg a special thermometer to help make the popular jasper ware.

Marketing

Wedgwood was an ambitious man. As he told a friend in 1775 he wanted to: 'ASTONISH THE WORLD ALL AT ONCE, for I hate piddeling you know.'

Mainly Wedgwood was a brilliant entrepreneur and salesman. He organised his production well. He used only the best designs. The famous 'willow pattern' was a Wedgwood design. The quality of the pots coming out of the Etruria works was high, whether fine porcelain for the rich or ordinary earthenware for everyday use by the workers. He set up display centres in London and other great cities where only the finest ornamental china was on display, for sale only to the rich and titled. He used advertising to sell more of his wares. From 1771 he was using travelling salesmen equipped with a catalogue—in foreign languages too. People were anxious to buy from a potter who sold to kings and queens, and large quantities were exported to Germany, Ireland, Holland, Russia, Spain, the East Indies, America, and France.

It looked as if Wedgwood was already well on the way to his ambition to be 'Vase Maker General to the Universe' twenty five years before his death.

▶ What methods of selling used by Wedgwood are still in use today?

▶ What methods of selling used today were not used by Wedgwood?

Location

- ▶ What are kaolin and earthenware?

- ▶ Why was a canal an especially good form of transport for finished pots?

- ▶ When did Wedgwood die?

Cotton mills were sited in the hills as they needed fast-flowing water to drive the waterwheels. This was not the case with pottery. It had been discovered in the 1760s however that white Cornish clay, or kaolin, could be mixed with china stone to produce porcelain. Porcelain was fine, high quality pottery, that was being demanded increasingly as the country became more prosperous, and the fashion grew for drinking tea and coffee. It was this use of kaolin that decided where Wedgwood's new factory was to be. Kaolin had to be brought from Cornwall to the Potteries and the best method was by water. James Brindley, who had built the successful Bridgewater Canal, began to build a canal linking the rivers Trent and Mersey in 1766. Wedgwood saw the possibilities and built his factory, and his house, on the banks of the new canal. Transporting kaolin would now be easy. Indeed Wedgwood felt this to be so important that he put a lot of his own money into financing this 'Grand Trunk' canal.

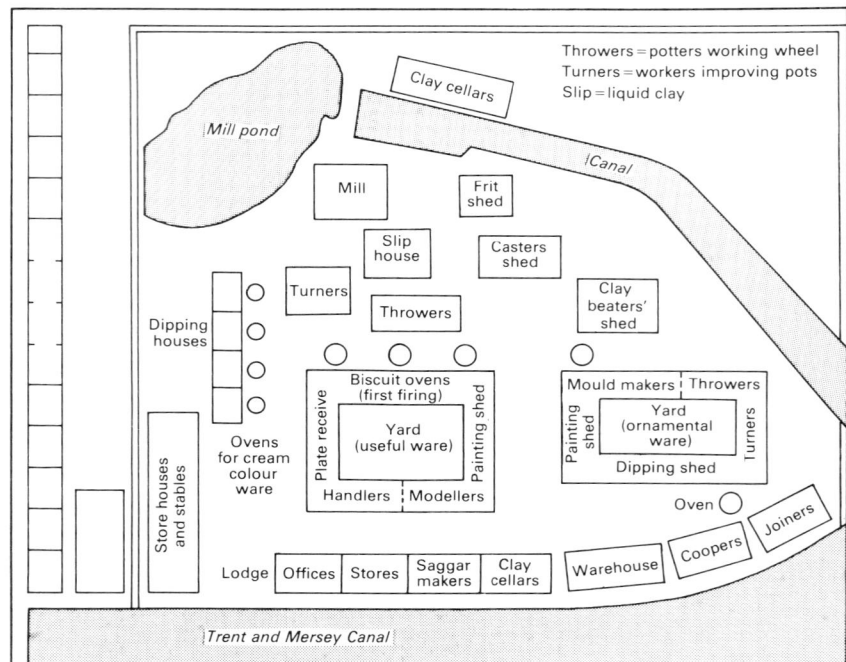

Questions

1. On a blank map of Britain, mark in Etruria, the sources of Wedgwood's raw materials, and the routes by which the raw material came to the factory.
2. If the kaolin from which the pots are made was found in Cornwall why not build the factory in Cornwall and save on transport costs?
3. Draw a map to show all the markets in which Wedgwood sold pottery. Show the routes by which the pottery would have travelled.
4. How far is it true to say that canals were crucial to Wedgwood's success?
5. The Concise Oxford Dictionary defines an obituary as 'Notice of death esp. in a newspaper, brief biography of the deceased person'.
   Write an obituary for a local Staffordshire newspaper on the death of Josiah Wedgwood.

6. Factories, as we know them, are the results of the work of three men, Richard Arkwright, Josiah Wedgwood and James Watt. Explain just what you understand by the phrase 'factory system' and explain how each of the three contribute to the development of the factory system. (You will need to refresh your memory of 'The Coming of the Factory', perhaps look at 'Early Factories 1'. James Watt is dealt with in 'Steam Power' p. 66.)
7. Find out how Wedgwood treated his workers. (Hint: He gave evidence to Peel's Committee on the Employment of Children in 1816. The evidence might be in your local library.)

Textiles

Key Ideas
1. The delayed impact of power looms
2. The development in wool was slower than cotton
3. Problems of a mixed system led to the heyday of the weaver

Core Skills
1. Chronology
2. Asking historical questions

Cotton

SOURCE 28 — The growth of cotton

From 1770 to 1788 a complete change had been effected in the spinning of yarns—that of wool disappearing altogether and that of linen was also nearly gone. Cotton, cotton, cotton, was become the almost universal material for employment. The hand-wheels, with the exception of one establishment, were all thrown into the lumber rooms. The carding for all numbers up to forty hanks in the pound was done on carding engines, but the finer numbers were still carded by hand . . . In weaving no great alteration had taken place in these eighteen years save the introduction of the fly shuttle.
(W. Radcliffe, 'Origin of the New System of Manufactures', 1828)

By 1800 the manufacture of cotton was highly developed. Spinning was already being carried out in factories (See 'The Coming of the Factory'), but there were further changes underway. The weavers simply could not keep up with the output of thread from the spinning mills.

SOURCE 29 — Looms

Some attempts have been made to work a number of looms together by machinery. The first was upon the introduction of swivel looms above thirty years hence, by Mr. Gartside, with a capital water-wheel at his factory near Garret-hall, now a very large one for cotton spinning by water.
(Sir F.M. Eden, 'The State of the Poor', 1797)

Pollard's cotton twist mill in Manchester.

► What is the value in today's money of the £5 notes that the Bolton weavers put in their hats?

► If there was such a shortage of weavers, why were the weavers not working hard all the time?

Population in Wiltshire

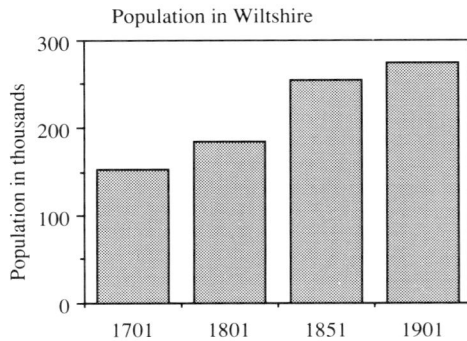

Population in West Riding, Yorkshire

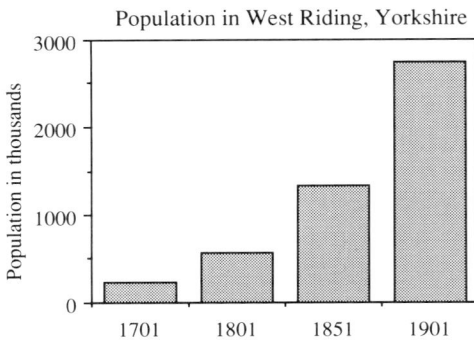

Population in Norfolk

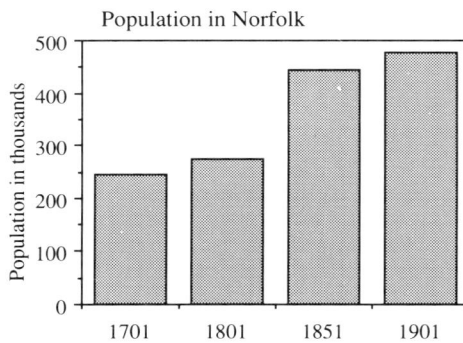

Population in Gloucestershire

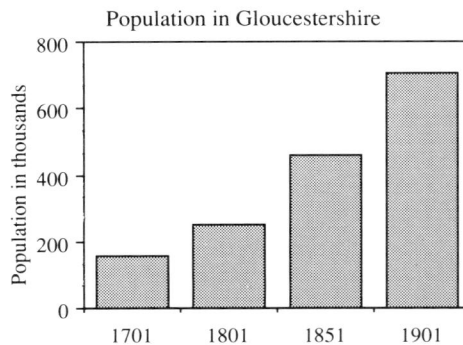

The growing population meant a demand for the cloth, there was plenty of thread, but not enough weavers. Those who could weave were paid enormous wages. Tales are told of weavers walking round Bolton with £5 notes stuck in their hatbands and using £1 notes to light their pipes. It was clear that power-looms were needed.

SOURCE 30
The weavers in a scarcity of spinning, have sometimes been paid less for the weft than they paid the spinner, lest their looms should be unemployed.
(Dr. Aiken, 'History of Manchester')

SOURCE 31 — The Spinner
It was no uncommon thing for a weaver to walk three or four miles in a morning, and call on five or six spinners, before he could collect enough weft to serve him for the remainder of the day; and when he wished to weave a piece in a shorter time than usual, a new ribbon, or a gown, was necessary to quicken the exertions of the spinner.
(R. Guest, 'History of the Cotton Manufacturer')

In 1785 Rev. Edmund Cartwright had invented a power loom. Power was provided originally by the weaver's feet and later by the new 'Boulton and Watt' steam engine. It was however both clumsy and inefficient. A factory was set up in Manchester in 1791 using 4000 power looms. It was burnt down, perhaps by handloom weavers who felt threatened. Nonetheless there was a clear need for the power loom. It was improved by William Horrocks in 1803 and by Richard Roberts in 1812. The power loom was here to stay, although the impact was much slower than that of the spinning machines. By 1840, except for a few highly specialised uses, the day of the hand loom was over.

The finishing processes were improved also. In 1783 Bell developed the use of copper rollers for printing cloth. Perhaps even more important was the use by Tennant of chlorine for bleaching cloth, a system which reduced the time needed to days instead of the months needed using the older methods. Mineral dyes began to replace the older vegetable dyes giving a greater range of colour.

Weaving by power loom.

Wool

Price for 24 yards of woollen cloth

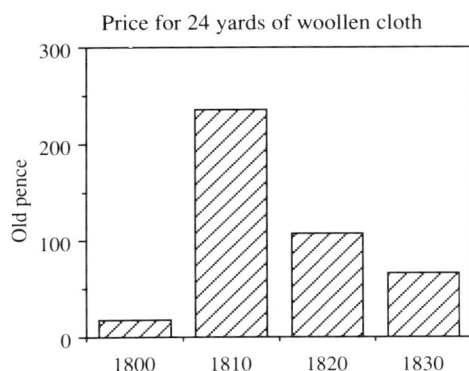

Number of factories in Manchester

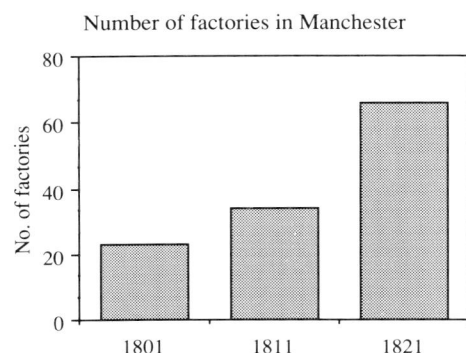

Problems

Power looms in Bradford

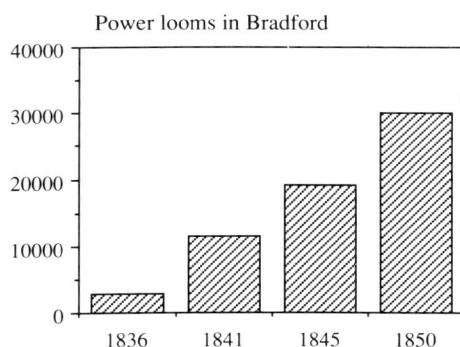

Number of factories, 1850

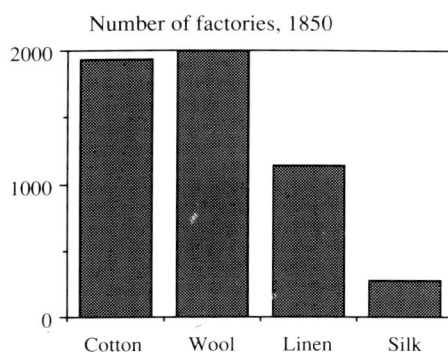

SOURCE 32 — The woollen industry

The Woollen manufacture, considering all its branches, is no doubt, a more important national concern than the cotton manufacture. It would seem, however, that the cottons of Manchester create more employment than the Norwich stuffs. The general languor of the woollen business seem to have been principally owing to the difficulty of introducing machinery.
(Sir F.M. Eden, op. cit.)

Changes in the woollen industry followed a similar pattern to cotton, although a little later. There were a number of reasons for the delay:

1. Production was more spread about the country, so ideas spread more slowly.
2. The curly woollen fibres were harder to work by machine than cotton ones. Cartwright had developed a combing machine, but it was not until Donisthorpe and Cunliffe-Lister's machine in 1861 that this problem was really solved.
3. There was plenty of skilled labour available.
4. There was a shortage of raw wool until Australian wool became available in the 1860s.
5. There were many rules and regulations governing wool, which was an old industry.
6. Many workers in Yorkshire were also independent farmers. They did not wish to go into factories and did not have the same need to do so.

Life for the hand loom weavers was a constantly changing one. For a few brief years it seemed there was an inexhaustible demand for the work of the hand loom weaver. There was a demand for cloth and the spinning machines were turning out huge quantities of yarn . . . Until the power looms came!

SOURCE 33 — The introduction of the power loom to Bradford

In and about 1826, power-looms were introduced into the town in considerable numbers. The riots which such introduction occasioned are before noticed. For a considerable time past, Bradford has been the great market for wool in the north of England.
(John James, 'The History of Bradford and its Parish', 1866)

SOURCE 34 — 'The Handloom Weaver's Lament'

And now, my lads, for to conclude,
its time to make an end;
Let's see if we can form a plan
that these bad times may mend;
Then give us our old prices,
as we have had before,
And we can live in happiness,
and rub off the old score.
(Sung by John Grimshaw, Abbey Wey, Gorton, Lancs. Probably dates from c. 1820)

SOURCE 35 — The weaver's workload

When I was young, Monday was generally regarded as a day of rest; Tuesday was not severe labour; Saturday was a day to go to the warehouse, and that was an easy day for the weaver. It is as much as we can do now, working hard all the week, and sometimes on Sunday besides, to be able to get a bare living: and such work so many hours destroy their health and strength.
(John Duce, Evidence to the Handloom Weavers' Commissioners, 1840)

SOURCE 36 — Power loom operators

People who blame handloom weavers for being obstinate and not taking jobs in the factories do not understand the problem. It is well-known that power looms do not need an adult worker, but they are managed entirely by young women and girls. There is no room for the male handloom weaver. The factories are closed to him.

(R. Gaskell, 'The Manufacturing Population of England', 1833)

SOURCE 37 — Titus Salt's new woollen mill

Saltaire is situated about four miles from Bradford in the beautiful valley of the Aire. Offices are now being built, facing the new road built by Mr. Salt which commences close by the Bingley turnpike-road, crosses the railway, the river and canal by two iron bridges.

When the works are finished, 4500 hands will be required to keep them going. The weaving shed will contain 1200 looms; the length of the shafting will be 9870 feet; the steam engines to work these shafts are equal to 1250 horse-power.

(*The Illustrated London News*, 1st October 1853)

Saltaire, Titus Salt's woollen mill in Yorkshire.

▶ How do you think Saltaire got its name?

▶ List all the reasons why Saltaire was a good site for a mill.

▶ How does the fact that silk was a luxury trade stop it becoming a major industry like wool or cotton?

▶ Which woollen area grew in importance during the early nineteenth century? Which declined in importance?

The other textile trades of England continued. Linen developed, especially in Scotland and Northern Ireland. The silk trade grew, indeed it was in silk that the first spinning mill in the country was built, by Thomas Lombe in 1721, but it was a luxury trade. The hosiery industry became mechanised in the area around Nottingham. Nothing however came near to the spectacular progress made by the 'big two'.

Questions

1. Draw a time chart with two columns. In one put developments in the cotton industry, in the other put developments in the woollen industry.
2. Make two lists to show the advantages and disadvantages of mechanisation in the textile industries.
3. The new technology brought prosperity first for the handloom weavers and then poverty. Explain how this came about.
4. The growth of textiles in Lancashire and Yorkshire came about due to a number of factors: the presence of coal, soft water, major ports (eg Liverpool and Hull), fast-flowing streams, and a workforce skilled in making textiles. Explain why each was important. Add any other factors you can think of. Which do you think were really important and which less so? Were the different factors more important at different times? Explain.
5. Can you think of any areas that are developing or declining today due to changing technology. Make two separate lists.
6. Find out who Jacquard was. What did he do for the textile trades?
7. EITHER
   Write a brief biography of Titus Salt. Was he like, or unlike, other mill owners? Explain.
   OR
   Compare Titus Salt and Josiah Wedgwood. In what ways were they similar and in what ways different?
8. Explain how and why the trade of handloom weaving declined. It might help to refer back to earlier chapters on early factories.

Iron

Key Ideas
1. Types of iron
2. Change of fuel/change of location
3. Line with water power
4. New technology meant larger units
5. New products

Core Skills
1. Chronology
2. Language
3. Historical Ideas
4. Asking Historical Questions

Process and product

Iron works were usually found where there was iron ore and timber for charcoal close together to avoid expensive and difficult transport problems, and also fast-flowing streams. Water power was important in the production of iron. It did two things:

a. Drove the bellows which blew air through the furnaces, increasing the heat.
b. Worked the heavy hammers used in forging.

► Why were ponds and pools so important to the iron industry?

SOURCE 38 — The iron industry
(Sussex) is full of iron mines, all over it; for the casting of which there are furnaces up and down the country, and abundance of wood is yearly spent; many streams are drawn into one channel, and a great deal of meadow ground is turned into ponds and pools for the driving of mills by the flashes, which, beating with hammers upon the iron, fill the neighbourhood round about it, night and day with continual noise.
(Camden, 1850s)

Iron making was a domestic industry and most workers combined two or more jobs, eg farmer and weaver. This went right up the scale and masters too often had different business interests. One man in Gorton, near Manchester, was farmer, carrier and undertaker. Thomas Harrison and his brother John were nailmasters at Belper. Thomas went to London to sell nails.

SOURCE 39 — A letter from Thomas Harrison to his brother
Have they finished getting out the potatoes? Has Joseph been paid and did you remember the milk? Chas. must pull the turnip field enough to supply the cows with tops. Had you many nails in on Monday? Mour and Co. say they are buying lighter nails out of Staffordshire. As far as I can at present judge am afraid shall not have many orders.
('The Harrison Papers')

When Joseph Walker, Nailer, of Stubben House, in the parish of Ecclesfield died in 1729 an inventory of his goods was taken in the normal manner.

	£	s	d
IMPRIMIS, his purse and apparell	3	0	0
One Range one pr of Tongues 3 Iron potts		12	0
Settle One dresser	1	1	0
In ye Smith. 1 pr of Old Bellows & all other work tools		10	0
2 Old Carts 1 plow 3 Horses with Gears belonging to them	18	0	8

▶ Rewrite the inventory of Joseph Walker (Source 40) in modern English. Change the money into modern money. You might be able to work out how much the same things would cost today.

The tools with which to make nails were hardly expensive—less than the price of a fireplace, pair of tongues and 3 iron pots. This was making nails in the backyard. It worked in a similar fashion to the domestic system in the textile trades. When the nails had been made they would be taken to somebody like the Harrisons, who would pay for them and provide iron for the next batch.

There are several stages involved.

Charcoal

It was the branches of trees, or cordwood, that was used for charcoal. They were cut up into pieces about 1 metre long and a fire was made of them. This fire was covered with turf or clay in order to stop too much air getting in. This was a slow process. It took five days to burn and three days more to cool down.

Charcoal burning.

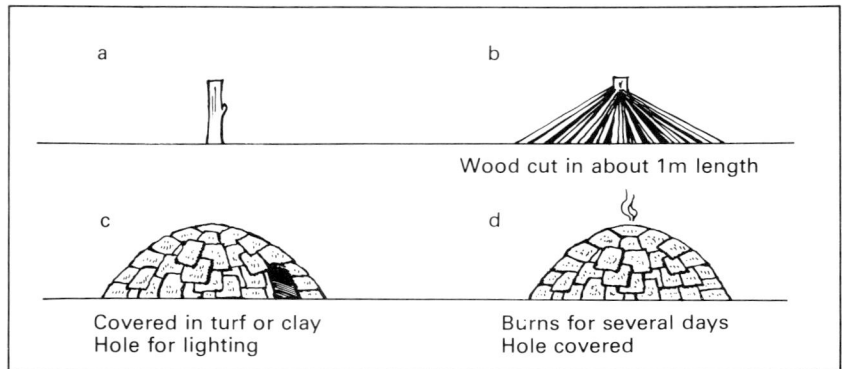

a

b

Wood cut in about 1m length

c

Covered in turf or clay
Hole for lighting

d

Burns for several days
Hole covered

It takes about an acre of wood to smelt a ton of iron. This fact in itself meant that furnaces had to be very small. If you built your furnace too big the problems of moving wood for great distances would become too great. The pattern was to have a small furnace and to supply it with local timber. The cordwood burnt very slowly indeed and left the charcoal behind. Trees in the area round a furnace were not just left to grow as they pleased but were 'farmed', using a system known as coppicing, and harvested regularly as any other crop.

Coppicing.

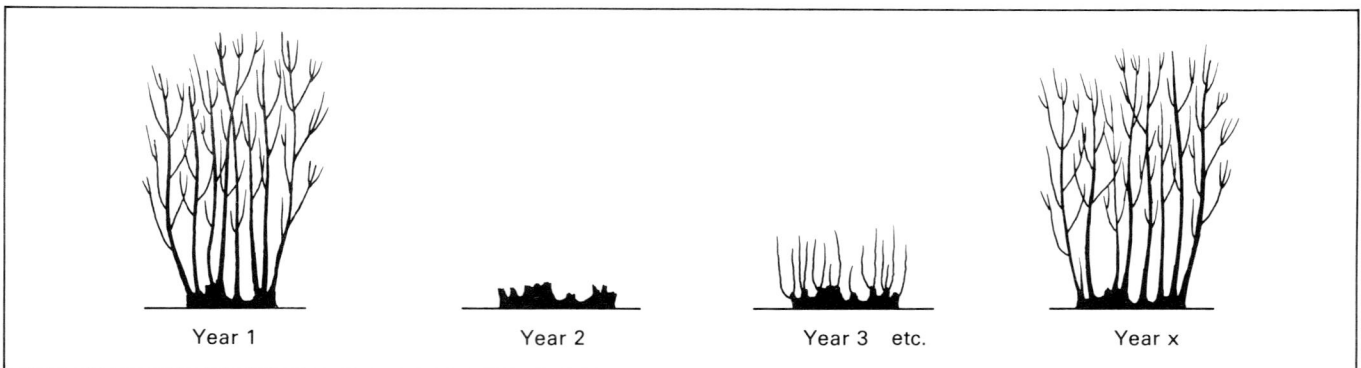

Year 1

Year 2

Year 3 etc.

Year x

Blast furnace

Charcoal and iron ore were put into a blast furnace and the charcoal was set alight. As the iron heated and melted it trickled down through the charcoal and collected at the bottom. There was waste called slag on the top. This was let out regularly through a tap part way up the furnace. When all the iron was smelted the tap at the bottom of the furnace was opened and the iron ran into moulds. These were in the shape of giant comb, called pigs or pig iron. Cast iron goods which were very hard, but also very brittle, were made by reheating the iron and letting it run into a mould of the shape you needed.

Blast Furnace.

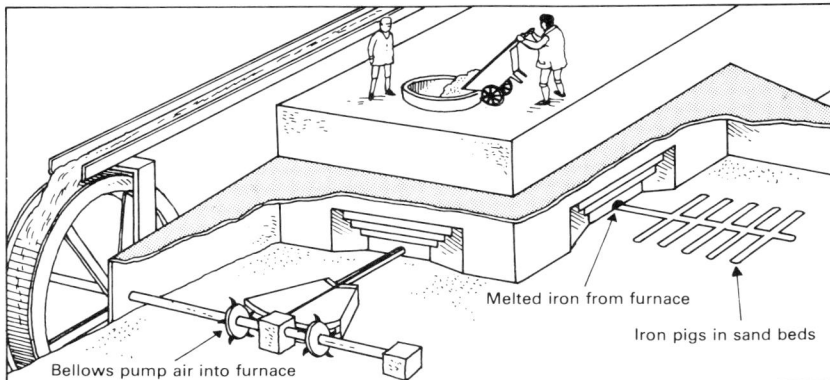

Bellows pump air into furnace

Melted iron from furnace

Iron pigs in sand beds

Iron has been made in significant quantities for some 4000 years, beginning in Asia about 1500 years earlier than in Europe. It was discovered that a bellows to blow air into the furnace increased the heat, and the blast furnace was developed, perhaps in what we would call Belgium. Casting was done in loam.

SOURCE 41
It was my husband's father (Abraham Darby) who was the first that set on foot the Brass Works at or near Bristol that attempted to mould and cast Iron pots etc., in sand instead of Loam . . . in which he succeeded. This first attempt was tryed at an Air Furnace in Bristol.
(A letter from Abiah Darby)

Even with the bellows the temperature was not very high. Abraham Darby III claimed that charcoal gave barely enough heat, with the result that the iron came oozing out of the furnace like toffee instead of running freely. You could make fire-back with it, but not a more complicated shape like a pot.

Forge.

Tilt hammers

Forge

This was the third stage in the production of iron. Pigs of iron were reheated and hammered, perhaps several times. This drove out the impurities and gave wrought iron which was less hard than cast iron, but also less liable to break. This hammering, or forging, was usually done by heavy tilt hammers driven by water wheels. Again bellows, often powered by water wheels, were used to raise the temperature inside the furnace.

The problem

SOURCE 42 — Large quantities of timber were used
I had the curiosity to see the great foundries, or iron works, which are carried on at such a prodigious expense of wood, that even in a country almost over-run with timber, they begin to complain of the consuming for those furnaces, and leaving the next age to want timber for their navies.
(Daniel Defoe, 'Tour through the Whole Island of Great Britain', 1726)

UK pig iron production

Year	
1910	
1900	
1890	
1880	
1870	
1860	
1850	
1840	
1830	
1820	
1810	
1880	
1790	

0   2000   4000   6000   8000   10000
Thousand metric tons

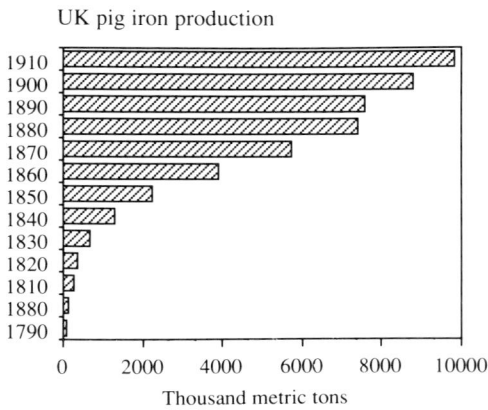

Production was less than 18 000 tons by 1740 and iron was being imported from Sweden, Russia and the American colonies. The main problem was the shortage of charcoal. Many books claim that there was a shortage of wood to turn into charcoal. This is what was said at the time (see Source 38). Experts today are less sure about this and feel that the shortage may have been due to some other cause.

Each small furnace, with its coppices round it, was self-sufficient and could go on producing indefinitely. The demand for iron was increasing and more furnaces would have to be set up. However there was plenty of wooded country still and, as T.S. Ashton commented in 'The Industrial Revolution', 'it was the presence of trees, rather than iron ore, that determined the location of ironworks'. Timber was being taken in increasing amounts for the navy, though this would have been a different type of timber altogether. It is difficult to be clear about the causes but two things are sure:

a.   Charcoal was essential to the production of iron.

b.   Charcoal was in short supply.

The answer

Although it was not realised at the time the answer was already in existence.

Abraham Darby, in 1709, found that coal could be used to smelt iron if it was turned into coke first. Strong blasts of air were needed in a coke furnace. This was only suitable for cast iron, being considered too impure for wrought iron. Darby made pots, kettles, stoves etc.

Abraham Darby II introduced limestone into furnace with iron ore and coke which improved quality of iron. He used a Newcomen steam engine to pump water back into the furnace pool for powering bellows, about 1742. Coal was coked in ovens, and not heaps like charcoal. Iron was now good enough for wrought iron.

Benjamin Huntsman, 1740, made steel by remelting iron in a clay 'crucible' and adding the correct amount of carbon. This was only suitable for producing steel in small quantities. Steel was very hard but tough and flexible and could be sharpened.

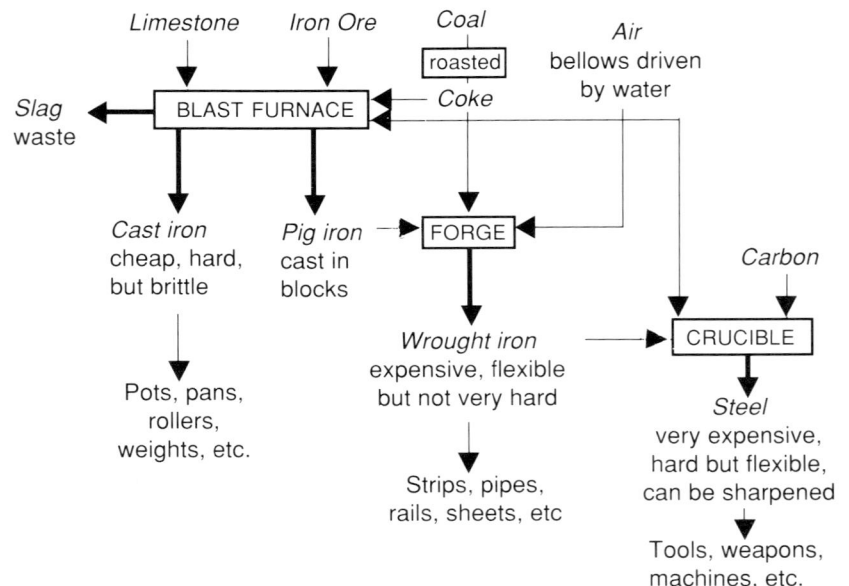

Iron and steel production around 1750.

► Find out about John Wilkinson and write an entry for 'Who's Who' about him.

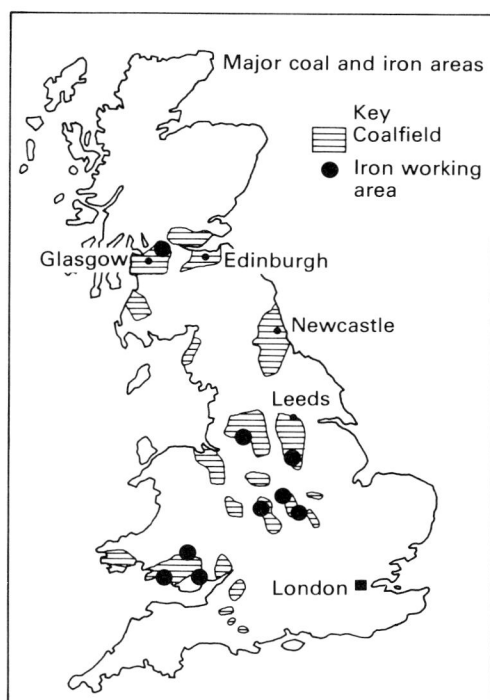
Major coal and iron areas

Key
Coalfield
● Iron working area

Glasgow ● ● Edinburgh
Newcastle
Leeds
London ■

► What was a reverberatory furnace? Try looking up 'reverberate' in a dictionary. Can you draw a diagram of one? You will have to find more information first.

► Make a time line to show the changes in the iron industry in the eighteenth century.

Steam engine factory and iron works, Bolton.

John Wilkinson, in 1775 used a Boulton and Watt steam engine to power bellows directly. He was known as 'Iron-Mad' Wilkinson as he used iron for everything.

Henry Cort, 1783, heated iron in a reverberatory furnace, which people had been experimenting with since 1766, and stirred or 'puddled' it while molten which drove out impurities. He rolled pig iron instead of hammering to give wrought iron. Charcoal not needed at all.

SOURCE 43 — The extent of the iron industry
The extent of the iron trade in all its varieties, wrought and unwrought, for agricultural and other internal purposes, and for home consumption and exportation, under its innumerable shapes and forms, is now so very great, as to rival that of the great staple, wool; and from the abundance of iron ore and fuel with which this country abounds, is capable of being much extended . . .
(W. Pitt, 'General View of the Agriculture of the county of Stafford', 1794)

James Neilson, 1828, heated air before it was blown through furnace. Coal consumption per ton of pig iron was reduced from eight tons to two tons. Coal no longer needed to be coked before using in the furnace.

SOURCE 44 — Iron
I admired, as in all the large factories I have had the chance of seeing in England, their skill in working iron and the great advantage it gives them as regards the motion, lastingness and accuracy of machinery. All driving wheels, and in fact almost all things, are made of cast iron of such a fine and hard quality that when rubbed it polishes up just like steel. There is no doubt but that the working of iron is one of the most essential of trades . . .
(A. & F. de La Rochefoucald-Liancourt, 'Voyage aux Montagnes', letter, 1786)

To produce iron in this quantity, and cast pieces of the size needed for huge driving wheels could not be done in small bloomeries. The furnaces used by the Darbys with waterwheels to provide the blast represented a huge amount of money. A large amount of investment was required to set up an iron works.

It was in the iron industry that vertical integration appeared. The larger firms began to control the complete process from raw material to finished product. Large companies such as the Crawshays of Cyfartha, in South Wales, mined their own coal and ore, smelted it, cast it, or rolled it into bars and forged it. The domestic system was dying.

▶ Find out what is meant by 'vertical integration' of an industry.

▶ In the early 1700s iron-masters wanted a site with iron ore, timber, and water. What three things were they looking for in a good site 100 years later?

The iron mining areas in South Wales.

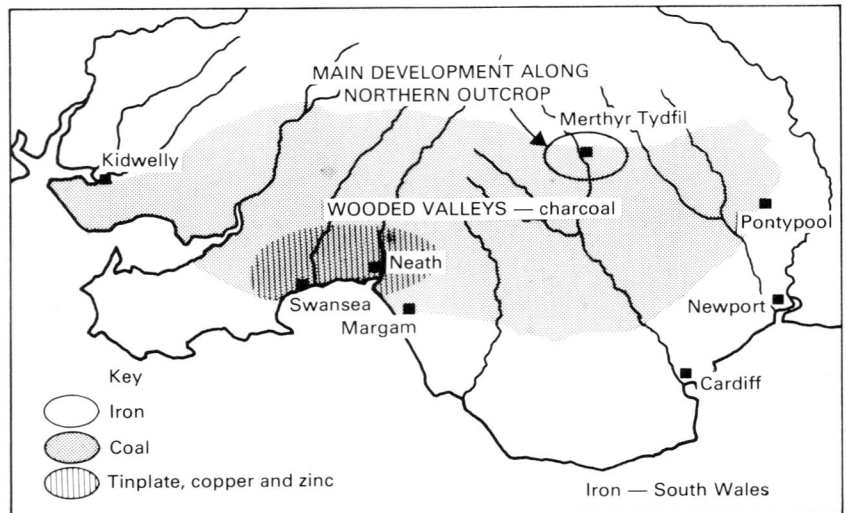

Iron — South Wales

Questions

1. What was the basic problem in the iron industry at the beginning of the eighteenth century?
2. To what extent do people of the time agree about the basic problem?
3. When, by whom, and how was it solved?
4. Below are a number of statements about the possible causes of a shortage of charcoal. Say whether you think each statement is: Unlikely, Possible, or Probable.
   Underneath each write a sentence to explain why you chose that particular grading.
   Statements
   Trees had stopped growing.
   Too much wood was being taken for shipbuilding.
   All the timber had been burnt.
   The demand for charcoal was growing.
   There was not enough charcoal burners.
5. About 1700 pots were cast in brass, not iron as they were later. What was the problem in trying to cast them in brass?
6. Why did Abraham Darby I's discovery solve this problem?
7. What were the results of coke smelting for the iron industry?
8. What were the results of coke smelting for Britain?
9. What new piece of technology was needed to develop the iron industry further?

Coalbrookdale — A Case in Point

Key Ideas
1. The impact of change on a place
2. The development of large scale industry
3. Location of industry

Core Skills
1. Chronology
2. Asking Historical Questions
3. Research
4. Empathy

Beginnings

A domestic industry was widespread in the West Midlands before 1700. Nails were made in backyard forges, the manufacture of locks was to develop in south Staffordshire. The area had the three prime requisites of the domestic iron trade—iron ore, supplies of wood and water-power to work the bellows.

SOURCE 45 — Abraham Darby I
About the year 1709 he came to Shropshire, to Coalbrookdale, and with other partners took a lease of the works which consisted of an old Blast Furnace and some Forges. Here he cast Iron Goods in sand out of the Blast Furnace that blow'd with wood charcoal; . . . Sometime after he suggested that it might be practicable to smelt the Iron from the ore in the Blast Furnace with Pit Coal; Upon this he tryed with raw coal as it came out of the Mines, but it did not answer. He not discouraged, had the coal coak'd into Cynder, as is done for drying Malt and then it succeeded to his satisfaction. He then erected another Blast Furnace and enlarged the works.
(A letter from Abiah Darby)

Neither Coalbrookdale, nor many other country areas were ever to be the same again. The iron was only suitable for casting. Only a certain type of coal gave the desired result. But improvements were on the way, even if the development did come slowly rather than a sudden dramatic change. Seventy five years later charcoal was finished in the production of iron.

Ironworks at Coalbrookdale.

The place

Coalbrookdale — an ideal setting for ironworks.

▶ Why would the River Severn be important in choosing a good site for Darby's ironworks?

▶ Many of Darby's products were sold in Britain. Why would this be a good market for Darby? Think of as many reasons as you can. Does the fact that they called their larger pots 'missionary pots' help?

▶ Can you find out any more about William Reynolds? You might try the 'Dictionary of National Biography' in your local library. It might be worthwhile designing a poster, or a wall display about him.

Diagram of the inclined plane.

Geographically many areas that had iron ore had coal also. Coalbrookdale was fortunate in this respect. Darby's discovery merely developed the area faster. His grandson, Abraham Darby III, was delighted, commenting that there seemed to be no limit to the amount of coal available and thus no limit to the amount of iron that could be produced.

He felt that Coalbrookdale 'was a good place for a furnace as it lay between the ore and the coal in the hills above, and the River Severn down below'. The raw materials came down the hill to the furnace, and then the castings went down the hill to the river. There was no need to haul heavy loads up steep slopes.

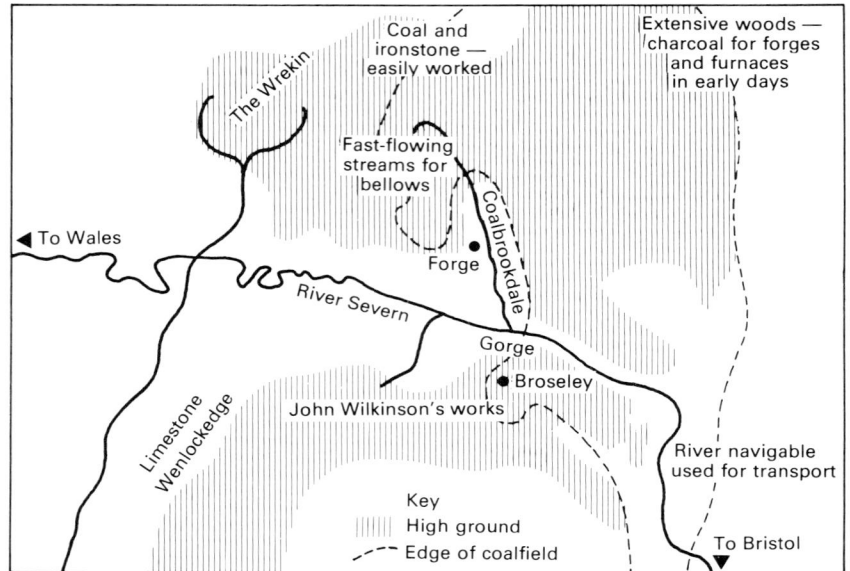

Other ironmasters were of the same opinion. John Wilkinson built at Brosely. William Reynolds was one of the partners at Coalbrookdale. In Coalbrookdale things were happening. Both Reynolds and Wilkinson made significant contributions to the development of the industry. Reynolds developed the inclined plane as a way of moving heavy loads, such as barges, from one level to another. Wilkinson made the first iron ship, he built an iron chapel, and had an iron coffin made for his burial. He developed a system for boring accurate barrels for cannon, which he used to make cylinders for steam engines. The steam engine blew the bellows on his furnaces.

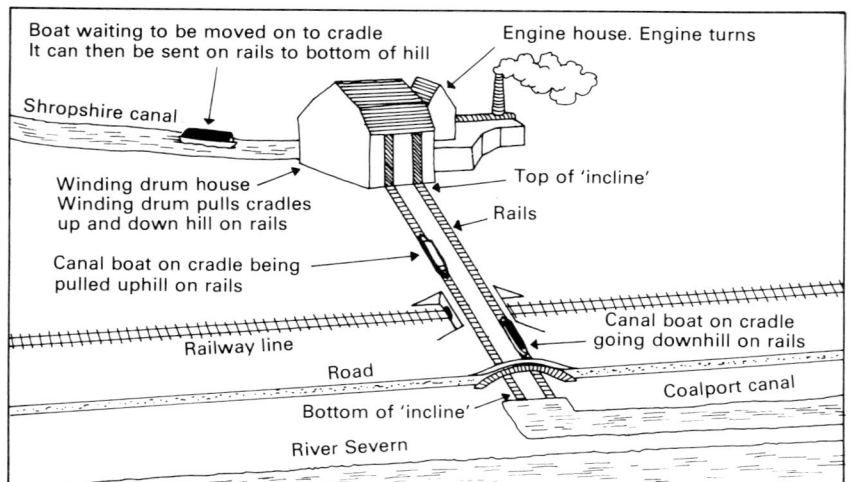

Problems

It was not before time. There were problems with water power. Richard Ford, a partner in the Coalbrookdale ironworks found out and recorded in his diary:- '12th July 1733—Yesterday was obliged to Blow out ye New Furnace our Water being quite gone.'

He was making the same complaint at the end of November:- '. . . there never was Such a Complaint at this time of ye year; but there is no remedy but Patience'.

By the 1740s Abraham Darby III was using a Newcomen engine to keep his ponds filled.

▶ What were the problems of using water power to drive the bellows?

Solutions

SOURCE 46 — Coalbrookdale was a source of constant development
He got roads laid with sleepers and rails. And one waggon with three horses will bring as much as twenty horses used to bring on horses' backs. Of late years the laying of the rails of cast iron was substituted; which, altho' expensive, answers well for Duration.
(A letter from Mrs. Abiah Darby)

▶ If each packhorse carried about ½ cwt, how much would three horses pulling a waggon be able to move?

▶ If cast-iron rails were so expensive, why were people prepared to use them?

The rails were originally made during a time of slack trade, rather than let the furnaces out and to keep the workers busy, rather than laying them off. The idea was that when times improved the rails could be taken up, remelted and cast, fairly quickly and cheaply. They did the job so well that they were never taken up. Rails were made for sale.

In 1779 the first iron bridge in the world was being built at Coalbrookdale by Darby, Wilkinson and others. It allowed the ironmasters to have easy access to the timber and limestone on the other side of the river. 'No one', said Abraham Darby III, 'has built an iron bridge before, but I am determined to try'. The sceptics claimed it would fall down. It didn't, and it drew people from all over the world, making a wonderful advertisement for iron, and for the Coalbrookdale iron masters.

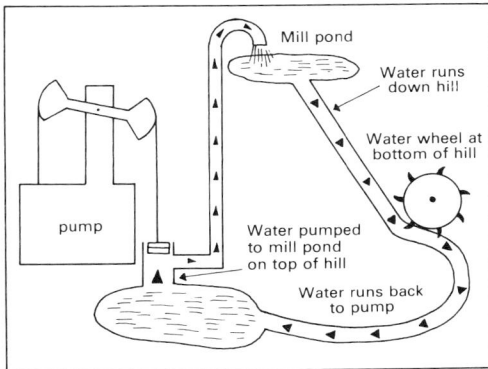

How Newcomen's engine was used.

The world's first iron bridge was built at Coalbrookdale in 1779.

Horsehay forge and rolling mill.

Decline

► Which countries were involved in the Napoleonic Wars? When did they end?

By the end of the Napoleonic Wars, Coalbrookdale seems to have been passed by. Developments were taking place elsewhere. A visitor to Darby's works commented that 'all the works seem to be conducted upon the old plans of forty years ago', and that 'all the machinery was old and clumsy'. South Wales, Staffordshire and other areas were in the ascendant.

SOURCE 47 — Industrial developments

About five miles from Newcastle are the ironworks, late Crowley's, supposed to be the greatest manufactory of its kind in Europe.
(Arthur Young, 1770)

All the way from Leeds to Sheffield it is coal and iron, and iron and coal. We saw the iron furnaces in all the horrible splendour of their everlasting blaze.
(William Cobbett, 1830)

The invention of the hot blast, in conjunction with the discovery of Black Band ironstone, has had an extraordinary effect upon the development of iron-manufacture in Scotland. By using the hot blast the coal could be sent to the furnace in its raw state. As fresh discoveries of the mineral were made, in Ayrshire and Lanarkshire, new works were erected.
(Samuel Smiles, 1863)

Questions

1. Darby, and many of the other Coalbrookdale ironmasters were Quakers. What are Quakers? What do they believe in? What kind of people are they usually?
2. In what ways was Coalbrookdale a good site for the manufacture of iron? You should consider all the information, not just one source.
3. Coalbrookdale was concerned with major developments in fuel, power and transport. What part was played in each of these?
4. Why did Darby's coke-fired furnace make only a limited change to the iron industry?
5. Look at the picture of the first iron bridge. In what ways might the shape of a modern iron (or steel) bridge be different? Why do you think the iron bridge was made in the shape it was? If you are not sure you might look at pictures of some older bridges.
6. On an outline map of Great Britain mark in the areas which took over from Coalbrookdale as major iron-producing areas.
7. In what ways would Coalbrookdale have changed over the hundred or so years between 1700 and 1810?
8. Imagine you were a farmer/nailer in Coalbrookdale in 1700. What happened to you when the Darbys came? How did you feel about it? Were you glad or sorry they were Quakers?

Steel

Key Ideas
1. Steel is better than iron
2. Growth of steelworks took place near the coast
3. British development led to the loss of British lead in this field

Core Skills
1. Comprehension
2. Asking Historical Questions
3. Historical Ideas
4. Research

A second industrial revolution

SOURCE 48

'The cost of making a steel rail was less than an iron one because it required less iron ore and less coal. He thought himself that a steel rail would last twice as long as an iron one.'
(Sir Lothian, Bell, evidence to 'Depression of Trade Commission', 1886)

The Crystal Palace designed for the Great Exhibition by Joseph Paxton was a triumph of the Iron Age. It was clear however that for many purposes steel was a better product than iron. It could however only be made in small quantities (See 'Iron'). The building of the railways in Britain had provided a huge demand for iron. The building of railways abroad would do the same. Steel could be better.

UK steel production (annual average over 10 years)

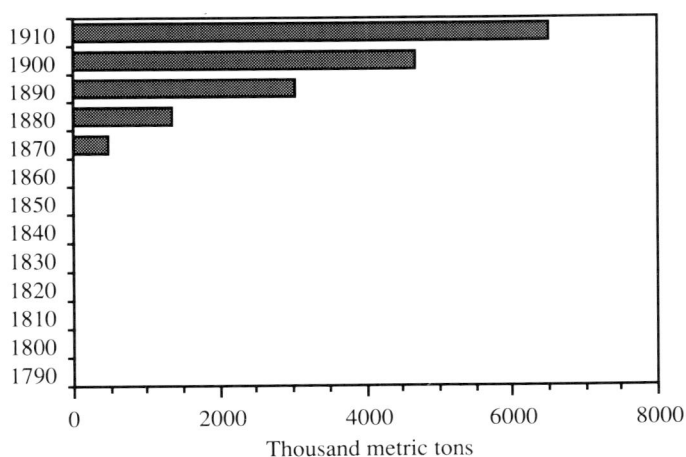

Steel

▶ What is an alloy?

Steel is an alloy of iron and carbon. So far it had only been possible to make it in small quantities at great expense. It was therefore used only where it was absolutely essential for tools, springs, weapons etc.

The breakthrough came in three stages. The first was by Henry Bessemer, a professional inventor, who devised the 'converter' (1856).

SOURCE 49 — Bessemer's converter

This new process of Mr. Bessemer's consists of merely forcing air through the molten pig iron. The molten iron is received red-hot into a sort of basin with holes at its bottom, communicating with a pair of very powerful blast-bellows, worked by steam. The air blast is turned on before the red-hot liquid is received into the basin.
(Chamber's Journal, 15th November 1856)

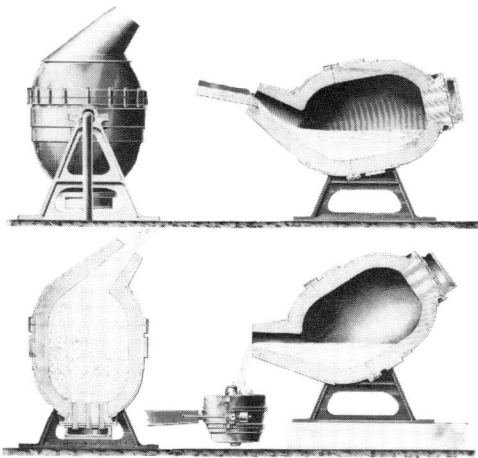

Bessemer's converter.

SOURCE 50 — Bessemer's account of the process

The oxygen, uniting with the carbon, sent up an ever-increasing stream of sparks and white flames. Then followed a series of mild explosions, throwing molten slag and splashes of metal high in the air, the machine becoming a real volcano in the state of eruption. No one could approach the converter to turn off the blast. In ten minutes more the eruption ceased, the flame died down, and the process was complete.

(Henry Bessemer, 1905)

The carbon in the iron was burnt, purifying it and at the same time increasing the heat. Finally small quantities of carbon and manganese were added to give mild steel. No fuel was needed and the process was quick. It was only necessary to 'blow' for some 15 or 20 minutes in order to turn pig iron into steel. Puddling was not needed and almost overnight the iron-puddling industry ceased to exist. There was still a problem. The process only worked with iron ores which did not contain phosphorus. The high quality iron ore of Cumbria did not.

SOURCE 51 — The ironworks at Barrow-in-Furness

The eleven large furnaces at Hindpool are capable of making iron at the rate of 500 tons a week each, at a price of £4 per ton. The steelworkers when in full operation would convert weekly about 1000 tons of pig iron into Bessemer steel, selling for about £12 or £14 per ton.

('Illustrated London News', 19th October 1867)

▶ How much pig iron did Hindpool make in a week?
How much did it sell as pig iron?
How much was the steel production worth?
What was the total weekly output of Hindpool worth?

Barrow-in-Furness iron and steel works, 1871.

Sidney Gilchrist Thomas and his cousin, Percy Gilchrist, lined the furnace with limestone. The limestone absorbed the phosphorous from the pig-iron and left behind calcium phosphate, which could be sold as a valuable fertiliser. British steel production grew from under 2 million tons between 1880 and 1884 to 7 million tons between 1910 and 1914. Steel works no longer had to be on the coast, and the phosphoric ore of Britain became usable.

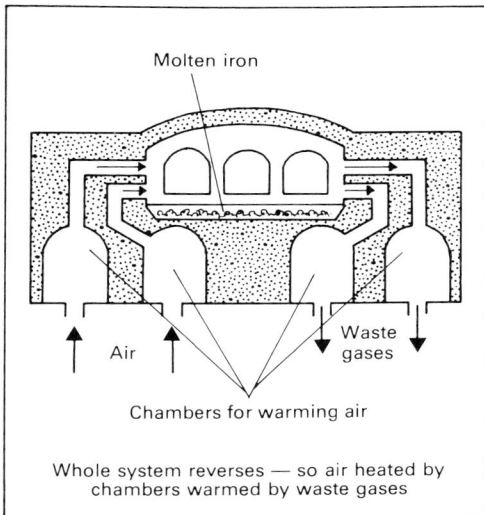

The open hearth furnace.

It took some years and the help of Robert Mushet to get rid of the phosphorous found in much iron ore. Only when this was done was the steel usable. Bessemer set up his own works in Sheffield in 1859. Steel making grew at Middlesborough, in the Scottish Lowlands, and in South Wales.

In the meantime, phosphorus-free ores had to be imported by those who wished to compete with works such as Hindpool. People had to import, for the Bessemer converter reduced the price of steel from some £60 per ton. Not only that but steel could be produced in large quantities, which it could not under Huntsman's method. Ore had to come from Sweden or Spain.

Iron continued to be used for many purposes for many years. It was still cheaper than steel, and the better wearing qualities of steel were not clear for some years. Nevertheless the price of steel dropped. It was used for railway axles, tyres, springs, rails, plates etc. Bessemer made profits of 100% every two months.

William Siemens, too, was a professional inventor, and an expert on saving fuel. He developed an 'open-hearth' furnace. The pig iron, or even scrap metal, was put into a small bath. A mixture of coal gas and air was burnt over it. This melted the iron and expelled the impurities. The key to the process was the high temperatures achieved, in part by using exhaust gases to heat the coal gas and air before it entered the furnace. The first commercial plant opened near Swansea in 1867.

▶ How long did steel rails last?

The open-hearth system was more reliable and easier to control. It was ideal for British use, especially as it could be used with quantities of steel which were too small to be worthwhile in the 'converter'. The fuel needed to produce a ton of steel dropped from 65 cwt of coke under the crucible process (See 'Iron') to 30 cwt of coal, and costs fell accordingly. Siemen's steel was felt to be more reliable than that of Bessemer for many purposes. The process was slow. It took from eight to twenty hours to make steel using the open-hearth system, but its main drawback was that it too could only be used with iron ore that was phosphorous-free. Nevertheless iron was on the way out. Iron rails on some railway routes were renewed every four months; steel rails could last twenty times as long.

SOURCE 52 — The age of steel
Manufactured iron. In our last circular we noticed the revolution produced in the rail trade by the adoption of steel instead of iron. This change has made further progress during 1878, to such an extent that many are exclaiming, 'The age of iron is passing away, and the age of steel has arrived.' Considerable attention is now being paid to steel plates for shipbuilding . . .
('Commercial History and Review of 1878', *The Economist*, 1879)

SOURCE 53 — Iron on the decrease

The prices of rolled iron have fluctuated during the last six months, and are now slightly higher than in the summer. They would be still higher but for the competition of steel, not only in shipbuilding, but in boilers, bridges and other structures. At many of the leading rolling mills Siemens and other steel-making plant has been established to meet the altered demand and at some works the puddling furnaces and other appliances for making wrought iron are likely to be abandoned altogether.

(*The Times*, 10th January 1887)

It was the solving of this particular problem that provided the third major breakthrough in the steel industry.

SOURCE 54

(Gilchrist and Thomas) were able to show the leading gentlemen of Middlesborough two successful operations on Friday, April 4th, 1879. The news of this success spread rapidly far and wide, and Middlesborough was besieged by the combined forces of Belgium, France, Prussia, Austria, and America.

(Richard Meade, 'The Coal and Iron Industries of the United Kingdom', 1879)

Unfortunately the discovery helped our competitors more than Britain. Countries such as Germany and the U.S.A. had huge quantities of phosphoric ores which they could now use. In addition they started to industrialise later than Britain. This meant that they were using the newest equipment while our equipment had been used for some years.

The development of other steels followed. In 1883 Robert Hadfield of Sheffield developed manganese steel, and later silicon steel. By 1913 stainless steel, an alloy of steel and chromium had been invented. The range of different steels for different purposes is now very wide indeed.

▶ Which industry was crucial in causing a general switch from iron to steel? Why was steel so much better?

▶ How many industries can you think of that would benefit from changing from iron to steel?

▶ Which foreign countries benefitted from the discoveries of Gilchrist and Thomas?

Questions

1. Explain why the steel industry moved to the coastal areas in the 1860s and 1870s?
2. If a Bessemer 'converter' took only 15-20 minutes and required no expensive fuel, why was it that the open-hearth system became more popular than the converter?
3. What changes did the invention of Bessemer and Gilchrist/Thomas bring about in the iron and steel industry? Outside the iron and steel industry?
4. Find out which steel-making areas developed after the Gilchrist/Thomas discovery. Why had they not developed earlier?
5. Explain how the discovery by Gilchrist/Thomas led to the decline in the British steel industry. (You will need to find out clear information as to which other countries developed, where and when.)

Engineering

A new trade

At the Great Exhibition in 1851 Joseph Whitworth of Manchester had no less than twenty three exhibits, including lathes, micrometers, planers and drills. He is best known for a revolutionary type of gun barrel and for classifying screw-threads. He followed a new profession that had not been known before the industrial revolution. He was an engineer.

The word itself tells us that the profession grew with the development of the steam engine. John Wilkinson was perhaps the first with a boring machine that made it possible to bore cylinders accurately. Steam engines and machines need parts that are exact copies of each other so that as one part wears out it can be replaced with another that is precisely the same. Even a skilled craftsman would find this difficult so parts had to be made mechanically. Machines had to be made to make machines. They were known as machine tools and they were the wonder of the world.

Soho Foundry, Manchester 1814.

SOURCE 55

To the ironmongers shops, which are greatly increased of late, are generally annexed smithies, where many articles are made, even to nails. A considerable iron foundry is established in Salford, in which are cast most of the articles wanted in Manchester and its neighbourhood, consisting chiefly of large cast wheels for the cotton machines; cylinders, boilers, and pipes for steam engines; cast ovens and grates of all sizes. This work belongs to Bateman and Sharrard, gentlemen every way qualified for so great an undertaking. Mr. Sharrard is a very ingenious and able engineer, who has improved upon and brought the steam engine to great perfection. There are five other foundries in Manchester, which do a great deal of business.

The tin-plate workers have found additional employment in furnishing many articles for spinning machines; as have also the braziers in casting wheels for the motion-work of the rollers used in them; and the clock-makers in cutting them. Harness-makers have been much employed in making bands for the carding engines.
(Sir F.M. Eden, 'The State of the Poor', 1797)

▶ What is a brazier? (NB Not the fire used by night watchmen and others.)

▶ How many old trades were involved in the development of engineering? Make a list of them.

The engineer clearly evolved from earlier trades such as carpenter and joiner, smith, clockmaker and millwright.

SOURCE 56 — The skill of the millwright

The millwright of former days was to a great extent the sole representative of mechanical art. He was a kind of jack-of-all-trades who could work at the lathe, the anvil or the carpenter's bench. He could handle the axe, the hammer and the plane with equal skill and precision: he could turn, bore, or forge with ease and despatch. Generally he was a fair arithmetician, knew something of geometry, levelling, and mensuration, and in some cases possessed a very competent knowledge of practical mathematics. He could calculate the velocities, strength, and power of machines; could draw in plan and section, and could construct buildings, conduits, or watercourses; he could build bridges, cut canals, and perform a variety of work now done by civil engineers.
(William Fairbairn, 'Treatise on Mills and Mill-work', 1861)

▶ Two types of engineering grew out of the millwright's craft. What do you think they were?

Early machines were hand-driven and made out of wood, but as machines became power-driven in factories they used increasing amounts of brass and iron, as did the water wheels and steam engines that provided the power. Engineering came to be associated with iron founding also.

▶ Early machines were made out of wood. Why were later machines made out of metal?

SOURCE 57 — Hand-made tools are inaccurate

When Sir Samuel Bentham made a tour through the manufacturing districts of England in 1791, he was surprised to find how little had been done to substitute the invariable accuracy of machinery for the uncertain dexterity of the human hand. As everything depended on the dexterity of the hand and correctness of eye of the workmen, the work turned out was of very unequal merit, besides being exceedingly costly . . . and but for the invention of machine-making tools, the use of the steam engine could never have become general.
(Samuel Smiles, 'Industrial Biography', 1863)

▶ What problems were caused by manufacturing machines by hand?

By 1811 the picture was already beginning to change. An American visiting Birmingham in 1811 recorded what he saw:

SOURCE 58 — Machine-made tools
Bars of iron, presented to the sharp jaws of gigantic scissors, moved by the steam engine, are clipped like paper. Iron-wire is spun out with as little effort than cotton thread on the jennies.
(Louis Simond)

SOURCE 59 — James Nasmyth's steam hammer exhibited at the Great Exhibition
The first hammer of 30 cwt, was made for the Patricroft works; and in the course of a few weeks it was in full work. The precision and beauty of its action were the admiration of all who saw it; and from that moment the steam-hammer became a recognised power in modern mechanics.
(Samuel Smiles, op. cit.)

SOURCE 60
While it is possible to obtain enormous impulsive force, it can be so graduated as to descend with power only sufficient to break an egg shell.
(Catalogue of the Great Exhibition, 1851)

By 1861 the situation was quite different.

SOURCE 61 — The Presidential Address to the British Association
Now, everything is done by machine tools with a degree of accuracy that the unaided hand could never accomplish. The automaton or self-acting machine tool has within itself an almost creative power; in fact so great are its powers of adaption that there is no operation of the human hand that it does not imitate.
(Wm. Fairbairn, Manchester, 1861)

The transition was the work of a remarkable group of men, who mostly had connections with each other.

John Wilkinson introduced accurate boring of cylinders for steam engines.

Joseph Bramah (1748-1814) was a carpenter and cabinet-maker who perfected a range of machine tools. He invented the hydraulic press, security lock (and the lathes to make it), water closet, beer-pump, and machine for printing serial numbers on bank notes. He invented or improved many useful devices.

Samuel Bentham developed wood-working machinery.

Henry Maudslay's two most important developments were a lathe to cut screws accurately and measurement to much finer tolerances than before. He also invented machines to make naval pulley-blocks and a slide-rest for lathes.

Joseph Clement worked on the domestic water tap and did much work on screw threads.

Nasmyth's steam hammer.

▶ Which machine, when it was invented, forced engineering to develop?

▶ Can you read the nameplate on the side of Nasmyth's steam hammer? Copy it out.

▶ Convert 30 cwt (30 'hundredweight') into kilograms.

Bramah's beer pump.

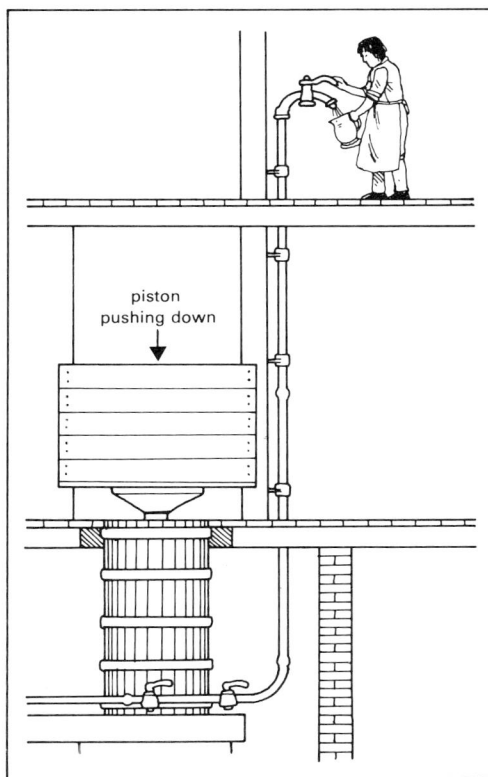

piston pushing down

Joseph Whitworth worked out a standardised system for classifying screw threads. His micrometer could measure to a millionth of an inch. He worked on the interchangeability of machine parts, self-acting planers, drillers, slotters, shapers. He had twenty-three exhibits at the Great Exhibition.

Whitworth's erecting shop, 1853.

Richard Roberts on request modified the spinning 'mule' to make it automatic. He was involved with lathes, metal-planing, gear-cutting, screw cutting and slotting.

James Nasmyth invented a safety ladle for molten metal, a series of precision, power-driven tools including shaper, planer, index miller and steam hammer.

In 1840 Henry Bessemer building machinery was able to order different pieces from different works and towns and know that when assembled they would all fit together—and work.

SOURCE 62

Where many counterparts or similar pieces enter into spinning apparatus, they are all made so perfectly identical in form and size, by the self-acting tools, such as the planing and key-groove cutting machines, that any one of them will at once fit into the position of any of its fellows in the general frame.
(Andrew Ure, 1835)

SOURCE 63 — Mass production was applied to engineering in Manchester

What might be called the straight line system has been adopted, that is the various workshops are all in line, and so placed that the work, as it passed from one end of the foundry to the other, received in succession, each operation which ought to follow the preceding one. By means of a railroad, any casting, however ponderous or massy, may be removed with the greatest care, rapidity, and security.

The whole of this establishment is divided into departments (which) may be thus specified:- The drawing office . . . then comes the pattern-makers . . . next comes the Foundry, and the iron and brass moulders; then the forgers or smiths. The chief part of the produce of the last named pass on to the turners and planers . . . Then comes the fitters and filers . . . in conjunction with this department is a class of men called erectors, that is, men who put together the framework, and the larger part of most machines.
(Love and Barton, 'Manchester As It Is', 1839)

Questions

1. In what ways would machines made in 1861 be better than those made in 1761?
2. EITHER:
   Design a poster to sell Nasmyth's steam hammer to industrialists in 1861.
   OR:
   Design a time chart for a classroom wall to show the changes in engineering.
3. Draw a plan of the works described by Love and Barton.
4. Write an essay to explain the development of the engineering industry. You will need to consider why changes were needed and what the changes were.
5. Most of these early engineers were connected as employers and employees. See if you can find out who employed whom at various times. (Hint: A good biographical dictionary might help.)

Shipbuilding

The old way

Ships were built where they were to be used and where the raw materials were readily available. For centuries this had meant that shipyards were scattered round the coasts of Britain. There was a shortage of timber (See 'Iron') even if not a shortage of wood for charcoal. Timber had to be imported from abroad. Iron, if used at all, was to cover a wooden frame with iron plates. Most ships were built out of timber. They were small. The largest ship in 1855 was only 3,600 tons.

The new way

There were already portents of change:

1788   Symington launched a paddle boat in Scotland.
1802   Symington's 'Charlotte Dundas' pulled two barges for 20 miles on the Forth-Clyde Canal.
1807   Fulton's 'Clermont', using a Boulton & Watt engine, sailed on the Hudson river in America.
1817   Steamboats running regularly on the Mississippi.
1818   US ship 'Savannah' crossed the Atlantic helped by steam.

Doubts

The 'Savannah' had only been helped by steam, though the 'Enterprise' did use steam for nine-tenths of the voyage a few years later. But what would happen if the engines broke down? Would the engines be jolted out of place in rough weather? Would the coal take up so much space that voyages would be uneconomic? Would ships be strong enough, or would the constant vibration from the engines shake the ship to pieces?

1838   'Sirius' and 'Great Western' crossed the Atlantic under steam. Francis Pettit-Smith's 'Archimedes' was the first successful screw-driven steamer.
1840   Samuel Cunard, of Nova Scotia, started the first regular line of ocean-going steamships.

John 'Iron-Mad' Wilkinson had pointed the way to the answer in 1785 for he had built an iron ship. To the surprise of everyone it had floated. By the late 1820s there were iron ships, though they were built on a wooden frame, and so were heavy and expensive to build. They gave rise to a new set of doubts. Iron corroded quickly in sea water. Iron quickly became encrusted with barnacles which slowed the ship down and thus required more fuel, and less cargo, to be carried. Nevertheless by 1837 the mail was being carried to Spain and Portugal by steam ship.

▶ Why were people fearful of steam ships? And iron ships?

50

Value of ships built and registered in the UK
(annual average over 10 years)

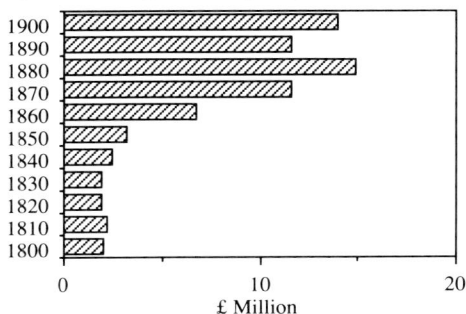

£ Million

▶ Why were propellers (screws) better than
paddle wheels?

A Newcastle shipyard.

▶ Look at the pictures of the shipyard. Are
the ships of wood or iron? Are they driven
by sail or steam? How can you tell?

Sunderland

Once ships were made entirely of iron they proved to be both stronger and lighter than wooden ones. They were therefore faster and needed less fuel. Larger ships were possible also with the added strength.

It was the flamboyant engineer Isambard Kingdom Brunel who led the way. In 1845 his 'Great Britain' crossed the Atlantic. It was driven by a screw, and it was made entirely of iron. In 1858 he launched the 'Great Eastern' of 13,000 tones. She was a commercial failure but a triumph of engineering and was the biggest ship afloat for forty years. She was eventually used to lay the first telegraph cable across the Atlantic.

The 'clippers', American-built with the unlimited supplies of cheap ship-building timber, held off the all-metal ships for a while. Cheap iron, and later cheap steel, however, coupled with the speed and reliability of the steam engine, made the new kind of ship inevitable. The fate of the clipper was sealed when Parsons invented the steam turbine in 1884, a new type of steam engine against which the clipper could not compete.

The change was slow in coming. In 1850 only 9% of new vessels built were of iron, and it was not until 1883 that the tonnage of steam ships exceeded the tonnage of sailing vessels.

Sunderland was a typical shipbuilding town of the period. It was a boom town, making its money from shipbuilding and exporting coal from the Durham coalfield. Other industries developed to service these two; anchor and chain forging, ropemaking, sailmaking etc. New houses were being built quickly to cater for those who were coming in to work in the expanding shipyards.

51

NAME OF STREET OR HOUSE	NAME AND SURNAME	RELATION TO HEAD OF HOUSE	CONDITION	AGE M	AGE F	RANK, OCCUPATION OR PROFESSION	WHERE BORN
Aylmer St. 7	Robert J. Christie	Head	Married	28		Mariner	Scotland
	Mary A. Christie	Wife	Married		25		Durham, Bishopwearmouth
	Elizabeth Christie	Daughter			4		Durham, Bishopwearmouth
	Robert Christie	Son		1			Durham, Bishopwearmouth
	Jacob Gales	Brother		17		Shipwright Ap.	Durham, Bishopwearmouth
7	George Shevil	Head	MARRIED	28		Shipwright, Journeyman	Durham, Monkwearmouth
	Hannah Shevil	Wife	Married		32		Durham, Bishopwearmouth
	George Shevil	Son		5		Scholar	Durham, Bishopwearmouth
	Betsy Shevil	Daughter			3		Durham, Bishopwearmouth
	William Rochester	Lodger		26		Shipwright, Journeyman	Durham, Bishopwearmouth
Aylmer St. 8	William Wilkinson	Head	Married	32		Blacksmith	Durham, Bishopwearmouth
	Jane Wilkinson	Wife	Married		32		Durham, Bishopwearmouth
Aylmer St. 9	James Laidlaw	Head	Married	61		Bottlemaker	Northld, Wooler
	Ann Laidlaw	Wife	Married		59		Durham, Bishopwearmouth
	Hutchinson Lamb	Step Son	Unmarried	17		Bottlemaker (App)	Durham, Bishopwearmouth
	David Adams	Lodger	Unmarried	29		Carpenter	Surrey, Surreyside
	William Kosher	Lodger	Unmarried	17		Blacksmith (App)	Northld, Belford
Aylmer St. 10	Anthony Vasey	Head	Married	26		Carpenter	Durham, Sunderland
	Margaret Vasey	Wife	Married		22		Durham, Sunderland
	William Vasey	Son		3			Durham, Sunderland
	Margaret Vasey	Daughter			9 months		Durham, Sunderland
Aylmer St. 11	William Hindmarsh	Head	Married	32		Shipwright	Northld, N. Shields
	Jane Hindmarsh	Wife	Married		30		Durham, Bishopwearmouth
	William Hindmarsh	Son		11			Durham, Bishopwearmouth
	Mary Hindmarsh	Daughter			3		Durham, Bishopwearmouth
	John Hindmarsh	Son		2			Durham, Bishopwearmouth
Aylmer St. 12	Mary Rogers	Wife	Married		41	Mariner's Wife	Durham, Monkwearmouth
	Jane Rogers	Daughter			15	Dressmaker	Durham, Monkwearmouth
Aylmer St. 13	Ann Fuller	Wife	Married		34	Mariner's Wife	Durham, Sunderland
Aylmer St. 14	Edward Nettleship	Head	Married	41		Blacksmith	Durham, Sunderland
	Elizabeth Nettleship	Wife	Married		47		Northld, Milburn
	Eleanor Nettleship	Daughter			17		Durham, South Shields
	Sarah B. Nettleship	Daughter			7	Scholar	
Aylmer St. 15	William Bulmer	Head	Married	32		Sawyer	Yorkshire, Lyth
	Jane Bulmer	Wife	Married		32		Yorkshire, Whitby
	Richard Bulmer	Son		8		Scholar	Yorkshire, Whitby
	William Bulmer	Son		6		Scholar	Yorkshire, Whitby
Aylmer St. 16	Thomas Williams	Head	Married	36		Tailor	Durham, Bishopwearmouth
	Elizabeth J. Williams	Wife	Married		27		Durham, Lumley
	Elizabeth Williams	Daughter			8	Scholar	Durham, Lumley
	John Williams	Son		5		Scholar	Durham, Bishopwearmouth
	Sarah Williams	Daughter			3	Scholar	Durham, Bishopwearmouth
	Mary Williams						
Aylmer St. 17	William Jacques	Head	Married	51		Grocer and Brickmaker	Durham, Sadberge
	Ann Jacques	Wife	Married		51		Durham, Norton
	Christopher Jacques	Son	Widower	23		Brickmaker	Durham, Norton
	Isaac Jacques	Son	Unmarried	21		Baker	Durham, Norton
	John Jacques	Son	Unmarried	19		Shipwright (App)	Durham, Norton
	Mathew Rawling	Servant		15		Servant	Durham, Norton
	Mary Rawling	Servant			14	Servant	Durham, Norton
Aylmer St. 18	John Shoreland	Head	Married	62		Labourer	Ireland
	Ann Shoreland	Wife	Married		54		Ireland
	Peter Shoreland	Son	Unmarried	32		Sawyer	Ireland
	Edward Shoreland	Son	Unmarried	25		Labourer	Ireland
	James Shoreland	Son	Unmarried	18		Shipwrights (App)	Ireland
	John Shoreland	Son	Unmarried	15		Shipwrights (App)	Ireland
	Alitia Shoreland	Daughter	Unmarried		23		Ireland
	Catherine Shoreland	Daughter	Unmarried		9		Ireland
	Mary Shoreland	Servant	Unmarried		42	Servant	Ireland
	James Shoreland	Visitor	Unmarried	60			Ireland
Aylmer St. 19	John Levison	Head	Married	30		Shipwright	Durham, Bishopwearmouth
	Frances Levison	Wife	Married		29		Durham, Bishopwearmouth
	John Levison	Son		9		Scholar	Durham, Bishopwearmouth
	William Levison	Son		7		Scholar	Durham, Bishopwearmouth
	Sarah Levison	Daughter			5	Scholar	Durham, Bishopwearmouth
	Maria Levison	Daughter			3		Durham, Bishopwearmouth
	Arthur Levison	Son		6 months			Durham, Bishopwearmouth
Aylmer St. 20	Margaret Hunter	Head	Widow		45		Durham, Bishopwearmouth
	Mathew Hunter	Son		17		Shipwright (App)	Durham, Bishopwearmouth
	Thomas Hunter	Son		15		Bottlemaker (App)	Durham, Bishopwearmouth
	William Hunter	Son		12		Errand Boy	Durham, Bishopwearmouth
	Jane Hunter	Daughter			8	Scholar	Durham, Bishopwearmouth
	Ann Hunter	Daughter			6	Scholar	Durham, Bishopwearmouth
Aylmer St. 21	Thomas Dodd	Head	Married	30		Boot & Shoe Maker	Westmorld, Kirby Stephen
	Mary Dodd	Wife	Married		22		Durham, Bishopwearmouth
	William Dodd	Son		5		Scholar	Durham, Bishopwearmouth
	Hannah Dodd	Daughter			2		Durham, Bishopwearmouth
	John J. Dodd	Son		1			Durham, Bishopwearmouth
	Elizabeth Gregdon	Sister-in-law			13	Servant	Durham, Bishopwearmouth
Aylmer St. 22	Hannah Nairm	Head	Widow		53		Yorkshire, Whitby
	Ralph Nairm	Son	Unmarried	23		Shipwright	Yorkshire, Whitby
	John Nairm	Son	Unmarried	21		Shipwright (App)	Yorkshire, Whitby
	Hannah Nairm	Daughter			18		Yorkshire, Whitby
	William Nairm	Son		16		Shipwright (App)	Yorkshire, Whitby
	Elizabeth Nairm	Daughter			14	Servant	Yorkshire, Whitby
Aylmer St. 23	Patrick Raffet	Head	Married	26		Labourer	Durham, Bishopwearmouth
	Mary Raffet	Wife	Married		28		Durham, Bishopwearmouth
	Thomas Raffet	Son		3			Durham, Bishopwearmouth
Aylmer St. 24	Thomas Doughan	Head	Married	27		Brickmaker	Ireland
	Jane Doughan	Wife	Married		28		Durham, Bishopwearmouth
	Sarah Doughan	Daughter			7	Scholar	Durham, Bishopwearmouth
	Eliza Doughan	Daughter			4		Durham, Bishopwearmouth
Aylmer St. 24	Alexander Reed	Head	Married	37		Joiner	Durham, Bishopwearmouth
	Mary Reed	Wife	Married		26		Durham, Bishopwearmouth
	Thomas Reed	Son		3			Durham, Bishopwearmouth
	John Reed	Son		1			Durham, Bishopwearmouth
Aylmer St. 25	John Locke	Head	Married	31		Glass Painter & Stainer	Cumberld, Carlisle
	Elizabeth Locke	Wife	Married		39		Scotland
	Ann Locke	Daughter			16		Scotland
Aylmer St.	George Locke	Son		14		Glass Cutter (App)	Durham, Hylton
	Elizabeth Locke	Daughter			9	Scholar	Northld, North Shields
	John Locke	Son				Scholar	
Aylmer St. 26	James Gregson	Head	Widower	44		Joiner	Durham, Benton
	Nicholas Gregson	Son	Unmarried	21		Shipwright	Durham, Bishopwearmouth
	June Gregson	Daughter			19		Durham, Bishopwearmouth
	James Gregson	Son		15		Blacksmith (App)	Durham, Bishopwearmouth
	Elizabeth Gregson	Daughter			12	Scholar	Durham, Bishopwearmouth
	William Gregson	Son		9		Scholar	Durham, Bishopwearmouth
	Thomas Gregson	Son		7		Scholar	Durham, Bishopwearmouth
	Robert Gregson	Son		5		Scholar	Durham, Bishopwearmouth
Aylmer St. 27	Thomas Sanderson	Head	Married	42		Shipwright	Durham, Monkwearmouth
	Elizabeth Sanderson	Wife	Married		42		Durham, Monkwearmouth
Aylmer St. 28	Ralph B. Simpson	Head	Married	35		Joiner (Blind)	Northld, North Shields
	Barbara Simpson	Wife	Married		34		Northld, North Shields
	William Simpson	Son		12		Scholar	Northld, North Shields
	John Simpson	Son		10		Scholar	Durham, Bishopwearmouth
	Ralph B. Simpson	Son		7		Scholar	Durham, Bishopwearmouth
	Jane Simpson	Daughter			3	Scholar	Durham, Bishopwearmouth
	Andrew Simpson	Son		1			Durham, Bishopwearmouth
	James Graham	Lodger	Unmarried	24		Schoolmaster	Durham, Hetton

Census for Aylmer Street, Sunderland, 1851.

▶ Draw a bar chart of the different occupations shown by the census.

▶ How many worked in the shipyards, or in related trades?

▶ How many were in service trades? Ask your teacher to explain a service trade if you do not know.

▶ Did most of the women work? What kind of women did work mostly? What does this tell you about the prosperity of Sunderland at this time?

▶ Were most ships built for sail or steam? How do you know?

▶ On a blank map mark where the workers came from to work in Sunderland.

Robert Thompson began building ships on his own account in 1854 at the Southwick Yard in Sunderland.

Output of Robert Thompson Jnr.

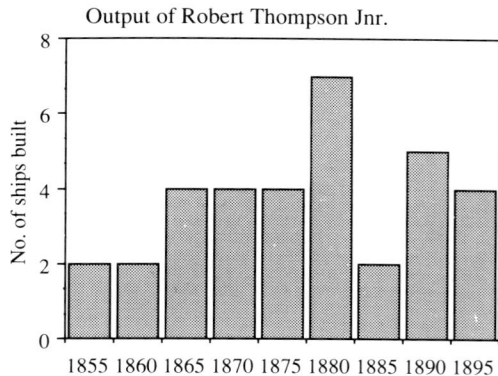

(Bar chart: No. of ships built vs years 1855–1895)

SOURCE 64 — Entries in Robert Thompson's books

Last Wood Vessel built by Robert Thompson Jnr.
No. 23 "Gitanella" 1865

First Composite vessel built by do.
No. 24 "Southwick" 1865

Last Composite vessel built by do.
No. 78 "Helma Mena" 1876

First Iron Vessel built by do.
No. 37 "Ireshope" 1863

Largest Wood vessel built by do.
"Solway" 176.8×33.3×22.1 946 tons nett. built 1857

▶ What do you think is meant by a composite vessel?

Robert Thompson Jnr. was a typical small shipbuilders of the period, building a handful of ships each year.

Shipping built for British users

▶ What other major industry was there in Deptford?

Deptford, Southwick and part of Sunderland, 1857.

Southwick and the River Wear, 1857.

Questions

1. Write a feature article for your school magazine on clippers. Why were they built? Where did they mostly sail? What routes did they take and why? Can you find any pictures? Can you find a newspaper report of the tea clippers racing to Britain with the first of the new crop from China? (Your local library might be able to help.)
2. What is a turbine and how does it work?
3. Explain how and why the location of the shipbuilding industry changed during the nineteenth century. Why was Sunderland in a good place using the old methods? Why was Sunderland in a good place using the new methods?
4. Describe a walk along the riverside in Southwick during the 1850s. You should use as many of the sources as possible to help you. You could draw a sketch map of your route. You could describe sights and sounds. You could also describe your feelings at being part of such a town.

Coal

Key Ideas
1. Only deep-mined coal could meet the demand
2. Deep-mined coal was impossible without technology
3. The problem of transport

Core Skills
1. Language
2. Synthesis
3. Asking Historical Questions
4. Chronology

1700

Coal shipped from Newcastle to London

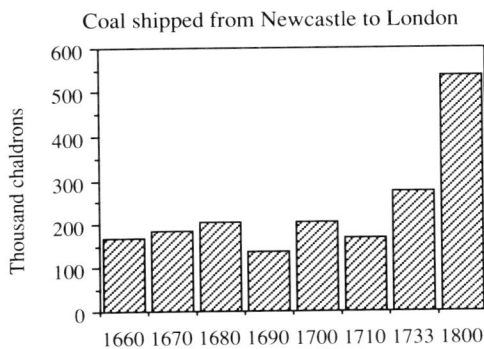

Why do you think it was called 'sea-coale'?

Coal was mined in all the present coalfields by 1700. It was in use in a number of industries—metal working, brewing, soap boiling, sugar refining, brick making—as well as for domestic use. This use was local apart from coal mined in the Northumberland and Durham area, which went by sea to London. Wood was too expensive, and too scarce to burn. By 1661 John Evelyn was complaining about 'the hellish and dismal cloude of sea-coale'. All these added together only demanded an output of some 2.5 million tons. The situation was to change dramatically. Wood was in short supply, the demand for coal went up for all industry and for domestic use. There were two other major changes also in the use of coal, or coke—to smelt iron and the development of the steam engine. The demand for coal rocketed.

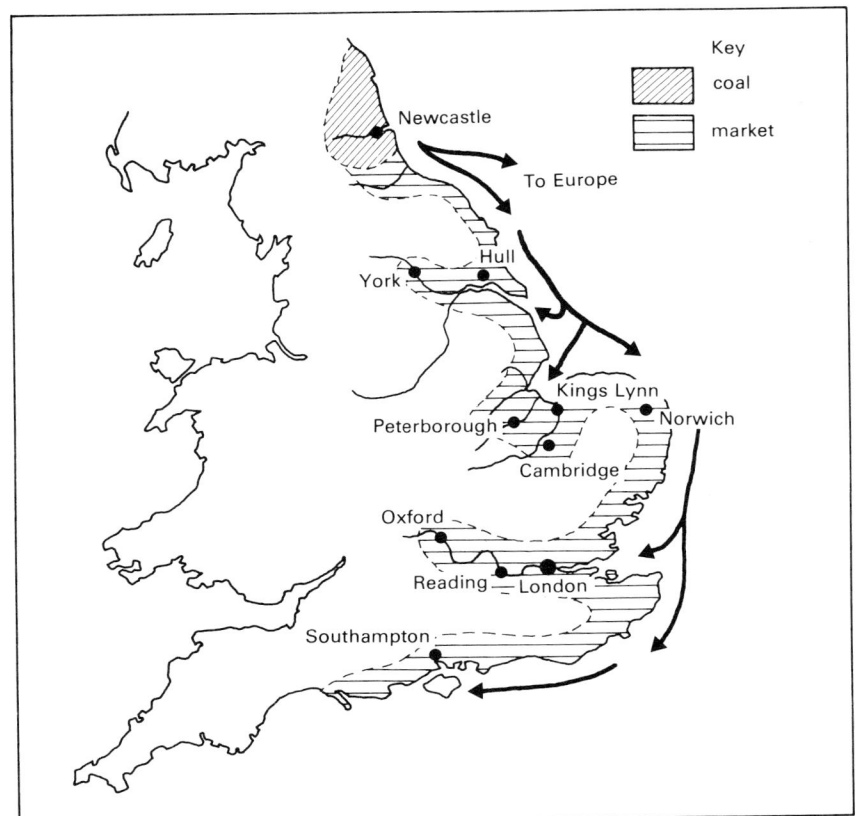

Coal shipped from Newcastle.

Gosforth Colliery.

Coal was mined by hand in one of two ways, the bell pit and the drift mine or adit.

Bell pit

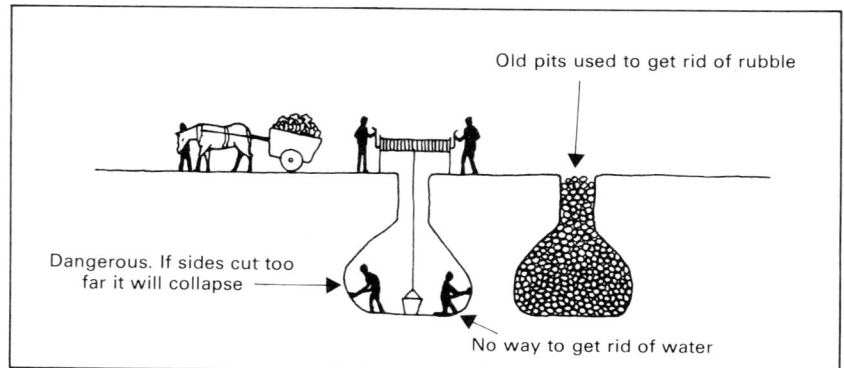

Old pits used to get rid of rubble

Dangerous. If sides cut too far it will collapse

No way to get rid of water

Adit

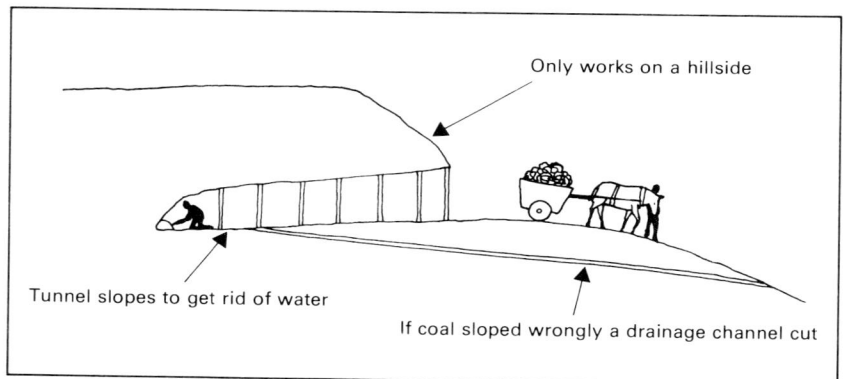

Only works on a hillside

Tunnel slopes to get rid of water

If coal sloped wrongly a drainage channel cut

▶ What were the main difficulties in mining by bell pit and adit?

These small pits could not meet the demand. The only answer was to dig deeper pits and to spread out further from the shaft. This led to further problems, lifting coal up deep shafts and gas. As pits got deeper pillars of coal were left to support the roof. Roof falls were common. Pits acted as a giant sink and filled up with water. Adits were not too bad. You might be able to dig slightly upward so the water drained out; you might at least be able to dig a sloping drainage channel; but bell pits were a problem.

SOURCE 65 — Gins

(They) . . . have great wheels that are turned with horses that draw up the water and so draine the Mines which would else be overflowed so as they could not dige the coale.
(Celia Fiennes, 'Diary of a Journey Through England on a Side Saddle', 1697)

They could also be used to lift people or coal.

A horse gin, which was used to drain the mines and to lift coal or people.

In fact deep mined coal would not have been possible at all had it not been for Newcomen's steam engine. It was used to refill the pool at Coalbrookdale. It had been built to pump out Cornish tin mines. It would pump out coal mines too.

SOURCE 66

You have a candle stuck into a bit of moist clay. With this your eyes become accustomed to the gloom and you can now explore the mine.
(John Randall, 'Shrewsbury Chronicle', 1859)

It is a bit surprising to find this system of lighting as late as 1859 but it was common in tin mines, lead mines and all other mines where gas was not a problem.

SOURCE 67 — The dangers of candle lighting

October, (1782)—An explosion of gas took place in Wallsend colliery, by which one man lost his life. The coal being set on fire, the colliery was drowned up to extinguish it.

November, (1784)—An explosion took place in Wallsend colliery, by which three men lost their lives. Another explosion occurred in December, when two men lost their lives. These explosions were supposed to have taken place at the spark of the steel mill, by the light of which the people were working in the shaft.
(John Sykes, 'Local Records', c.1830)

▶ Why was a candle not a suitable means of light for deep pits?

You can almost hear the disbelief that the steel mill could possibly have caused the explosion. The steel mill was a rough steel wheel turned by a handle. As the wheel was turned it rubbed against a flint and gave out a shower of sparks. By the light of these sparks men attempted to see. This was so inadequate that many still preferred to use candles. Seven months later there was no doubt.

SOURCE 68 — Wallsend colliery explosion

June, (1785)—An explosion occurred in Wallsend colliery, by which one man lost his life. This was the first explosion which was distinctly known to have taken place at the steel mill. Some doubt remained up to this time as to whether fire-damp would explode at the spark of the steel mill or not. John Selkirk, who was 'playing' the mill at the time, survived the accident.
(John Sykes, op. cit.)

SOURCE 69 — Felling Colliery

The working or down-shaft is called the John Pit. It is 204 yards deep, and furnished with a steam engine for drawing the coal. And with a whim gin, wrought by horses, of use in letting down and drawing up workmen when the machine chances to be crippled, or repairing.

The up-shaft, or air furnace shaft is called the William Pit. It is distinguished by a whim gin and a lofty tube of brickwork.

Trapdoors are placed to divert the air through proper channels. In all large collieries the air is accelerated through the workings, by placing a large fire, sometimes at the bottom, and sometimes at the top of the up-shaft, which in these cases is covered over and connected with a chimney.

If the air be conducted through all parts of the mine, as here described, and no falls from the roof occur each part of the mine will be wholesome . . . but when the fire is neglected or the trap doors are left open accumulations of fire-damp commence. Blasts occur in stagnations (of fire damp).
(A Description of Felling Colliery, Previous to May 25, 1812)

With the gas being sucked straight onto a furnace it is a miracle that there weren't more explosions. Part of the answer at least was not long in coming.

SOURCE 70

What is the deepest pit you know?
. . . 180 fathoms of shaft; but they frequently go deeper.
Generally what is the expense incurred in sinking a pit?
. . . upwards of £30 000; that includes the machinery for sinking that pit and the steam engine; that is merely getting to the coal.
Have you any calculations of the men and ships on the two rivers (Tyne and Wear)?
. . . seamen 15 000, pitmen and above ground people at collieries 21 000, keelmen, coal boatmen, casters and trimmers, 2 000, making the total number in the Northern coal trade, 38 000.
Do you think that accidents by explosions have been lessened by Davy's safety lamp?
. . . They have. If we had not had the Davy lamp, these mines could not have been in existence at all. It costs only about 5 or 6 shillings. This introduced a new era in coal mining.
(J. Buddle—Evidence to the House of Lords 1829)

Miners' safety lamps, invented by George Stephenson and Humphrey Davy.

Humphrey Davy and George Stephenson both invented safety lamps based on the same principle at more or less the same time in 1815.

A turn wheel in use.

SOURCE 71 — Joshua Biram developed another lamp at Elsecar Colliery

I accompanyed Mr. Stephenson and Mr. Wood down Killingworth Colliery to try Mr. Stephenson's first safety lamp at a Blower. When we came near the Blower it was making more gas than usual that I told Mr. Stephenson and Mr. Wood that if the lamp should deceive him we should be severely burned. So Mr. Wood and I went out of the way at a distance and left Mr. Stephenson to himself, but we soon heard that the lamp had answered his expectations.
(John Moody, 1815)

Davy became the better known in this respect, but Stephenson lamps were used commonly in the north-east. These at least helped, but as long as furnaces were used to ventilate mines explosions were likely.

SOURCE 72

Explosions from fire damp are common in deep mines. One which happened near Newcastle was very remarkable: 70 men were blown out of the pit and a large piece of timber about ten yards long and ten inches thick was blown a considerable distance and stuck into the side of a hill.
(Dr William Smellie, 'A Treatise on Coal Mines', 1769)

The shafts were no safer, and posed just as big a problem. It was no good getting coal to the bottom of the shaft if you couldn't get it to the top. The small pits could not even afford a horse gin.

Children carrying heavy loads of coal.

SOURCE 73

The turn wheel is certainly dangerous as you depend all the time on the man or woman who works it. As soon as (the people being lifted) arrived at the top, the handle was made fast by a bolt drawn from the upright post; the woman then grasped a hand of both at the same time and by main force brought them to land.
(Mr Scriver, 'Report of the Children's Employment Commission (Mines)', 1842)

SOURCE 74

David Pellet was drawn over the roller by his own uncle and grandfather just at the moment when a passing funeral caught their attention.
(Mr Scriver, 'Report of the Children's Employment Commission (Mines)', 1842)

SOURCE 75

On Friday last, a steam engine constructed upon Mr. Watt's new principles was set to work at Bloomfield Colliery, near Dudley. All the iron foundry parts (which are unparalleled for truth) were executed by Mr. Wilkinson; and all the small work, at Soho.
('*Birmingham Gasette*', 11th March 1776)

SOURCE 76

The coalmines in the neighbourhood of Newcastle are so numerous that they may be regarded as not only one of the immense magazines of England, but also as a source of profitable foreign commerce. The first mine I visited belonged to a private individual; it requires one hundred men to work it; thirty for work above ground and seventy in the pit: twenty horses live in this profound abyss, and drag the coal through the subterranean passages to the pit bottom. At a depth of one hundred and two feet the coal is found. The seam is five feet thick in some places but in general it is easy wrought. The mine has a large steam engine for pumping out the water, and at the same time working a ventilator to purify the air.
(B. Faujas de St. Fond, 'A Journey Through England and Scotland', 1784)

The problem of haulage underground has been solved, though it was to be many years before children were no longer used for the purpose.

SOURCE 77

They are then loaded again into a great machine called a wagon; which by means of an artificial road, called a wagon-way, goes with the help of but one horse, and carries two children, or more, at a time, and this, sometimes, three or four miles to the nearest river or water carriage they come at; and there they are either thrown into, or from, a great storehouse, called a steath, made so artificially, with one part close to or hanging over the water, that the lighters or keels can come close to, or under it, and the coals be at once shot out of the wagon into the said lighters, which carry them to the ships.
(Daniel Defoe, 'The Complete English Tradesman', 1842 Ed.)

The importance of coal is difficult to overestimate. Along with textiles and iron it was to prove the foundation of British prosperity for some 200 years.

▶ How many ways can you think of for getting coal up the shaft? What are they?

▶ Even when men and coal were hauled up the shaft by steam engine they sometimes fell off half way up the shaft. Why would this not happen today? What is the main invention that has stopped this happening? (Hint: It is not in the text but you have used them. They began to be used in pits about 1860).

UK coal production
(Annual average over 10 years)

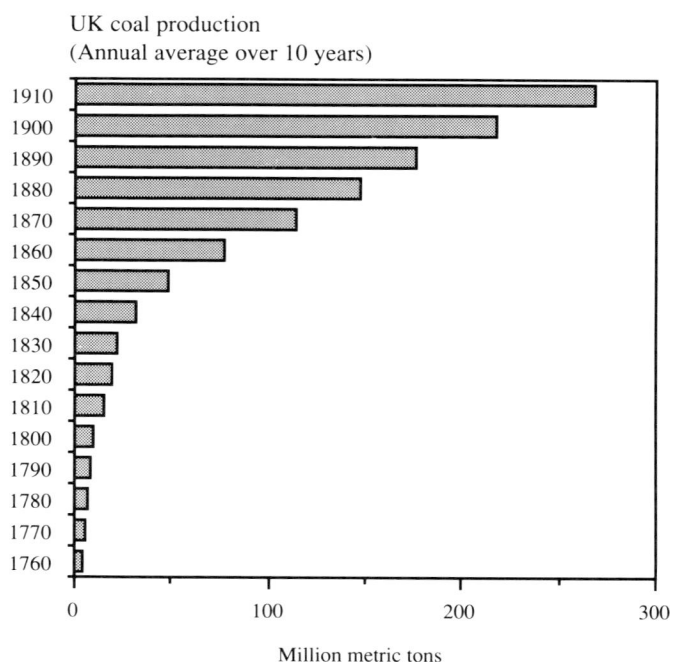

Million metric tons

SOURCE 78

From the activity of its manufactures and its commerce, Birmingham is one of the most curious towns in England. If any one should wish to see the most numerous and varied industries it is hither he must come. It is the abundance of coal which has performed this miracle and has created in the midst of a barren desert, a town with forty thousand inhabitants.

(B. Faujas de St. Fond, 'A Journey Through England and Scotland', 1784)

Winning coal however was never a safe occupation.

SOURCE 79 — Deaths in Coal Mines in Great Britain

Cause of Death	1838	1864
Explosion of Fire Damp	80	94
Falls in Mine	97	395
Falls of Items Down Shafts	4	51
Fell Down Shaft	66	64
Explosions of Gunpowder	4	15
Suffocation	8	8
Drowning	22	11
By Tram Wagons	21	56

Questions

1. Why was the coal industry in Northumberland and Durham bigger than that of any other area before 1700?
2. What problems might be caused by using:
   a. bellpits?
   b. drift mines?
   Which do you think is better? Explain your choice. If it was better, why was it not used all the time?
3. Explain the importance of the safety lamp in the development of the coal industry. Only one invention was as important, or perhaps even more so. What was it? Explain why it was so important.
4. What were the main problems in mining coal from deep mines? How were they solved?
5. Place the causes of death in order of importance (ie the highest numbers at the top of the list, lowest at the bottom). Was the order the same in 1864 as it had been in 1838?
6. Why do you think there were more deaths in 1864 than in 1838? Was it just bad luck? Had the colliers learnt nothing from past accidents? Or was there some other cause?
7. Draw a time line to show the major developments in coal mining.
8. How do the sources show that the pits were different during the early years of the 19th century from those at the time Celia Fiennes visited them in 1697?
9. What were the main uses for coal during the eighteenth century? How did this change as the century wore on?
10. What are
    staiths (steaths)?
    adits?
    steel mills?
    fire-damp?
    fathoms?
    whim-gins?

Water Power

Types of power

Power, as we know it, was unknown in 1700. There were only two sources of power available—muscle power, of man or animal, and the power of natural elements, wind or water.

Muscle power was used all the time, we even use it today. Wherever possible it made sense to use the muscles of animals rather than man. They tended to be stronger and to have more stamina. Horses and oxen were used to haul wagons and carts. Man was ingenious in converting animal power to be used in other ways. The horse gin allowed a horse to drive machines. (See 'Coal').

Wind power was used too. We have all seen pictures of windmills. The problem is that the wind does not always blow. Even in the high Pennines where the 'helm' wind blows very strongly it does not blow all the time. Wind power tended to be used mostly near the sea where there were no high hills to get in the way, places such as Lincolnshire and the Fylde coast of Lancashire. Even in a good breeze windmills did not give much more than 8 horsepower.

Far and away the most important source of power was water. Man had been using it for many years and had worked out elaborate systems for controlling it. Quarry Bank Mill, at Styal, near Manchester is a good example.

Water use at Quarry Bank Mill.

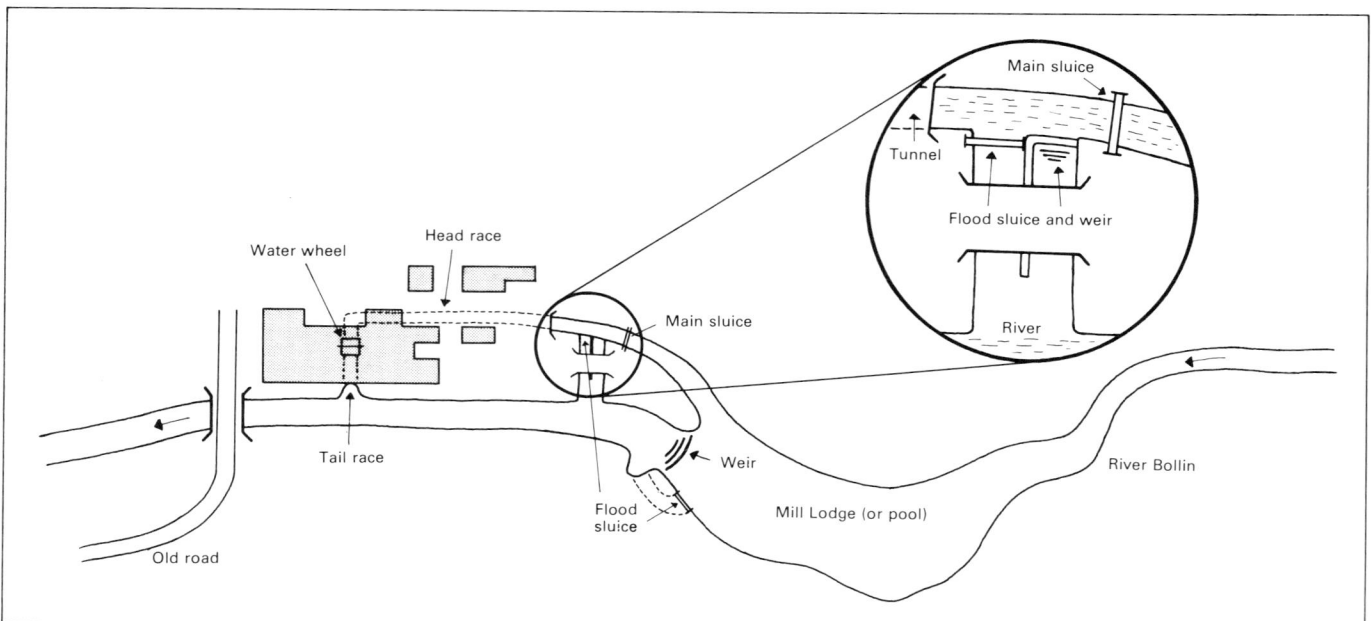

62

Killhope: a case study

Lead was mined at Killhope in Upper Weardale, in the high Pennines as it had been for centuries. From the day the new Park Level Mine opened in the 1850s until the day it closed in 1906 it was powered by water as lead mines always had been. It rains a lot in the high Pennines.

The most obvious use of the water was to power the great water wheel, which was 33 feet 8 inches in diameter, 6 feet wide, containing 74 buckets. It made 2 revolutions per minute and gave an output of 116 horsepower. This provided the power to haul the tubs of bouse (rock containing the lead ore) from the bousesteads where it was stored, up the incline, to the crusher. The water wheel provided the power to crush the bouse and powered the machinery which separated the lead ore from the waste rock. These worked on the principle that lead is very heavy. Crushed bouse agitated in water allows the lead to sink to the bottom and the lighter waste to go to the top. The lead could then be collected from the bottom. This would be done several times to ensure that all the lead was removed.

To ensure that no ore was lost accidentally, all water that had been used in the separation was taken to settling tanks. Any fine sediment was allowed to settle. The water was then drawn off and the sediment went to be separated yet again to make sure that no lead ore, or galena, was left. Even then the waste went to dolly tubs worked by hand for a final working to make sure that there were no remaining particles of lead.

Water underground was both a help and a problem. Water wheels were used underground as well as on the surface. They provided power for pumping with hydraulic engines and in some mines were used for winding.

▶ What is lead used for today? Can you find anything that it was used for in the 19th century that it is not used for today?

▶ What are 'hydraulic' engines?

SOURCE 80 — A 15 year old boy describes what it was like underground

'It was warm, but sometimes very bad for air; we can hardly breathe; they put pipes, and water comes down and great air comes up out of the water.'

The water wheel at Beamish Colliery.

Different types of water wheels.

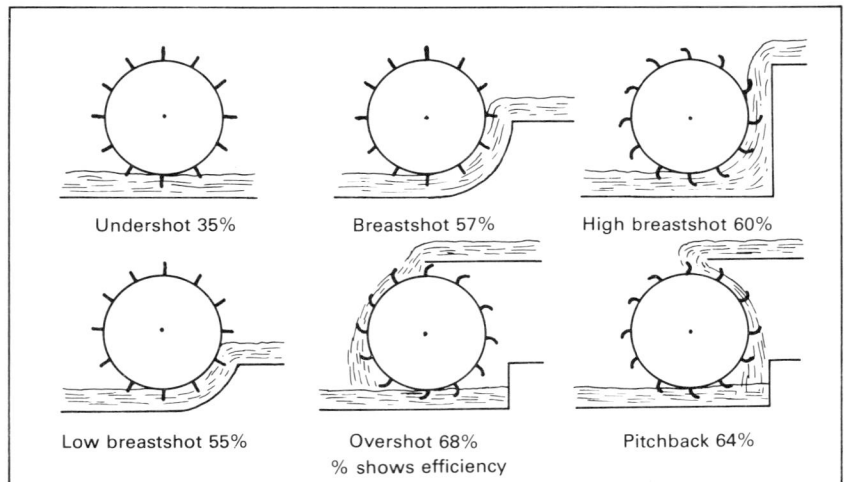

Undershot 35%   Breastshot 57%   High breastshot 60%

Low breastshot 55%   Overshot 68%   Pitchback 64%
                      % shows efficiency

▶ List the types of water-wheel in order of efficiency. Show the efficiency of each.

▶ What problems are to be found using water power?

The problem was to get rid of the water that was not needed. The mine was an adit (See 'Coal') and was known as a 'horse level' as horses drew the trams into and out of the mine. Water flowed out along the level. Hydraulic engines lifted water from lower levels to the horse level.

Water was powerful and had another use. When miners were searching for new veins of lead they would build an earth dam to create a reservoir of water. The water was released suddenly and, as it rushed down the hillside, it tore away soil, loose rocks etc. If a vein of lead was underneath it could then be seen. This process was known as hushing. Hushes, where this has been done, can still be seen in all the lead mining areas, e.g. Swaledale and Teesdale. They are long, steep-sided gashes on the hillsides but are now grown over with grass, bracken etc and to a casual glance resemble only a small valley.

Water was valuable. Even with an annual rainfall of some 63 inches there was rarely enough. It was so valuable that it was worthwhile to build channels or races to bring water to the crushing floors, and to build reservoirs to ensure a steady supply. Water for Killhope came from as far away as 9 miles. After Killhope had finished with it it went to be used again at Cowshill 3 miles away, and then to be used again at Westgate 5 miles further on again.

Date	Ore 000 tons	Lead 000 tons	Value £000s
1855	92.3	65.5	1517
1860	88.7	63.3	1413
1865	90.5	67.2	1433
1870	98.2	73.4	1453
1875	77.7	57.4	1290
1880	72.2	56.9	954
1885	51.3	37.7	433
1890	45.7	33.6	450
1895	38.4	29.0	309
1900	32.0	24.4	419
1905	27.6	20.6	286
1910	28.5	21.5	283
1914	26.0	19.4	372

▶ How much was each ton of finished lead worth in 1860, 1880, 1900 and 1914?

64

Water supply around Killhope

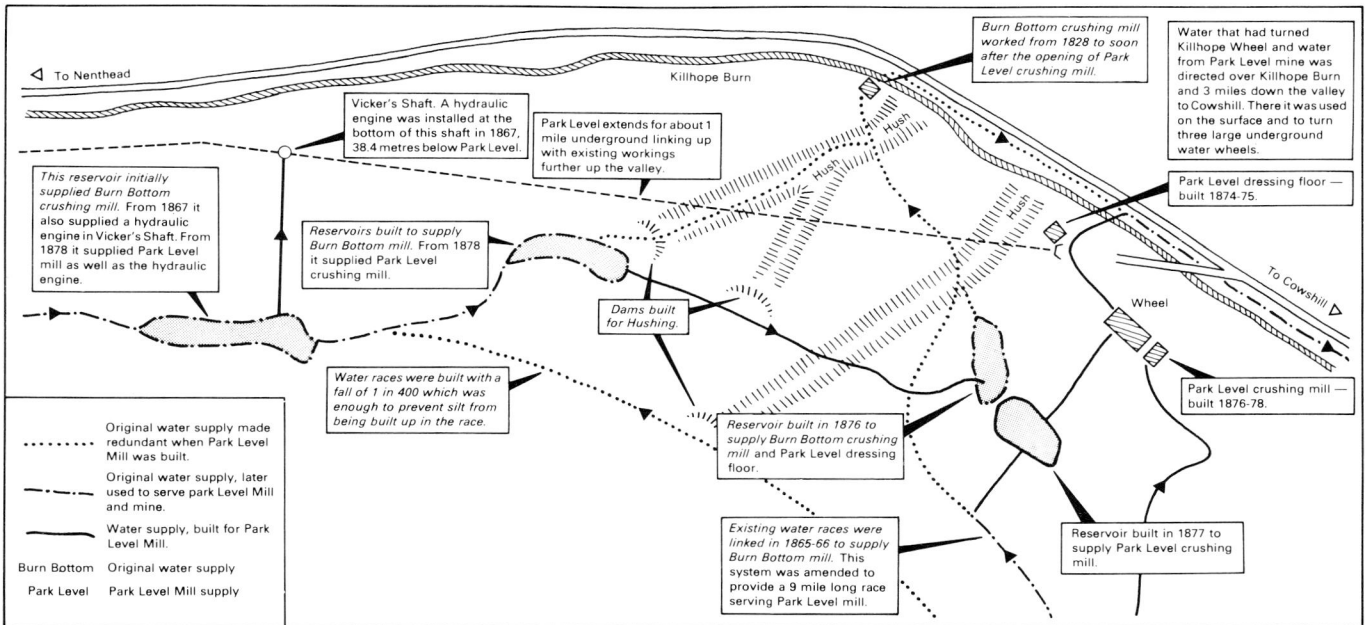

Map labels:

◁ To Nenthead

Killhope Burn

Burn Bottom crushing mill worked from 1828 to soon after the opening of Park Level crushing mill.

Water that had turned Killhope Wheel and water from Park Level mine was directed over Killhope Burn and 3 miles down the valley to Cowshill. There it was used on the surface and to turn three large underground water wheels.

Vicker's Shaft. A hydraulic engine was installed at the bottom of this shaft in 1867, 38.4 metres below Park Level.

Park Level extends for about 1 mile underground linking up with existing workings further up the valley.

This reservoir initially supplied Burn Bottom crushing mill. From 1867 it also supplied a hydraulic engine in Vicker's Shaft. From 1878 it supplied Park Level mill as well as the hydraulic engine.

Reservoirs built to supply Burn Bottom mill. From 1878 it supplied Park Level crushing mill.

Park Level dressing floor — built 1874-75.

To Cowshill ▷

Wheel

Dams built for Hushing.

Water races were built with a fall of 1 in 400 which was enough to prevent silt from being built up in the race.

Park Level crushing mill — built 1876-78.

Reservoir built in 1876 to supply Burn Bottom crushing mill and Park Level dressing floor.

Existing water races were linked in 1865-66 to supply Burn Bottom mill. This system was amended to provide a 9 mile long race serving Park Level mill.

Reservoir built in 1877 to supply Park Level crushing mill.

Legend:

.... Original water supply made redundant when Park Level Mill was built.

—·—·— Original water supply, later used to serve park Level Mill and mine.

———— Water supply, built for Park Level Mill.

Burn Bottom — Original water supply

Park Level — Park Level Mill supply

▶ What are:-
bouse?   galena?
hushes?   helm?
dolly tubs? sluices?
races?   bousesteads?

Park Level Crushing Mill.

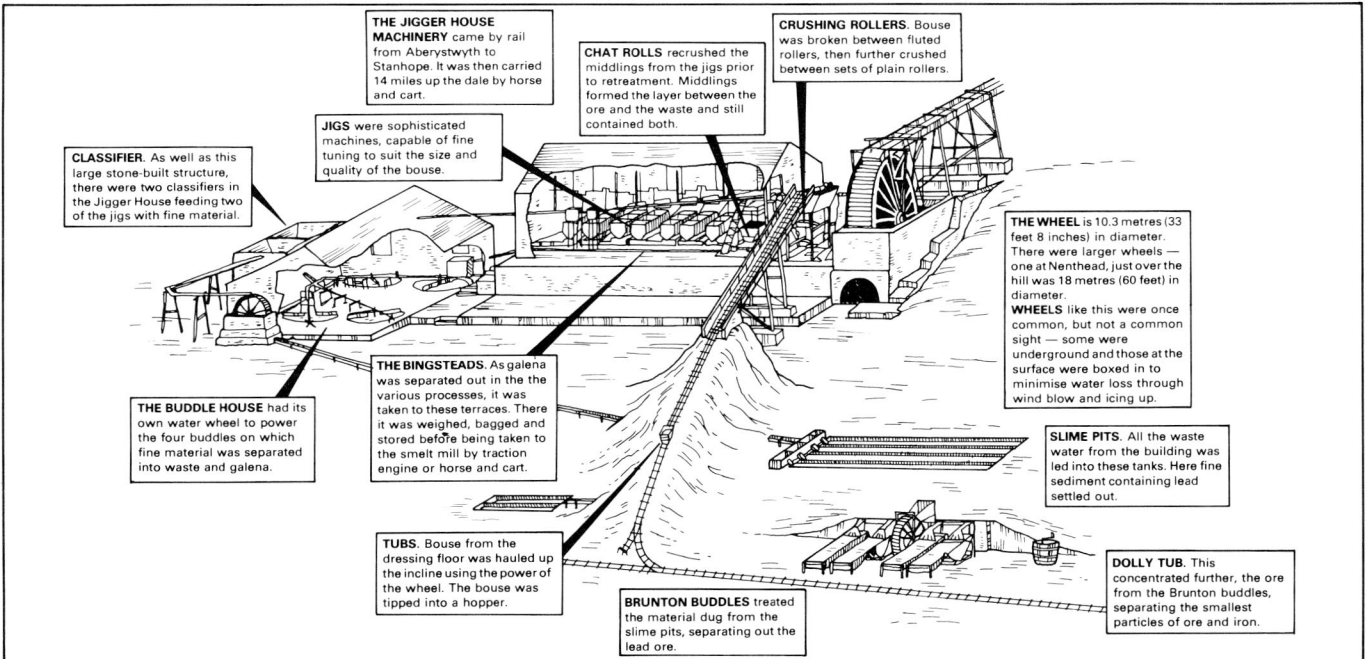

Diagram labels:

THE JIGGER HOUSE MACHINERY came by rail from Aberystwyth to Stanhope. It was then carried 14 miles up the dale by horse and cart.

CHAT ROLLS recrushed the middlings from the jigs prior to retreatment. Middlings formed the layer between the ore and the waste and still contained both.

CRUSHING ROLLERS. Bouse was broken between fluted rollers, then further crushed between sets of plain rollers.

JIGS were sophisticated machines, capable of fine tuning to suit the size and quality of the bouse.

CLASSIFIER. As well as this large stone-built structure, there were two classifiers in the Jigger House feeding two of the jigs with fine material.

THE WHEEL is 10.3 metres (33 feet 8 inches) in diameter. There were larger wheels — one at Nenthead, just over the hill was 18 metres (60 feet) in diameter.
WHEELS like this were once common, but not a common sight — some were underground and those at the surface were boxed in to minimise water loss through wind blow and icing up.

THE BINGSTEADS. As galena was separated out in the the various processes, it was taken to these terraces. There it was weighed, bagged and stored before being taken to the smelt mill by traction engine or horse and cart.

THE BUDDLE HOUSE had its own water wheel to power the four buddles on which fine material was separated into waste and galena.

SLIME PITS. All the waste water from the building was led into these tanks. Here fine sediment containing lead settled out.

DOLLY TUB. This concentrated further, the ore from the Brunton buddles, separating the smallest particles of ore and iron.

TUBS. Bouse from the dressing floor was hauled up the incline using the power of the wheel. The bouse was tipped into a hopper.

BRUNTON BUDDLES treated the material dug from the slime pits, separating out the lead ore.

Questions

1. Park Level Crushing Mill, where the Killhope Wheel is situated opened in the 1850s. Why do you think that they did not use steam power instead of water? Use the information in this and other chapters. Give as full an answer as you can.

2. Draw a sketch map to show the layout of Park Level Crushing Mill. Show the buildings, and what they were used for; the route taken by the bouse, and what happened to it; the route taken by the water, what it was used for, and the wheels.

3. Draw graphs to show the output of lead ore, the output of finished lead, and the value of the finished lead. Begin in 1850 and finish in 1914.

4. If some water wheels are more efficient than others, why were they not built all the time and the old designs ignored altogether?

5. Mills such as Quarry Bank used water power right into the 20th century. Water wheels were eventually replaced by turbines. What were turbines and how did they work?

Steam Power

Key Ideas
1. Large amounts of power
2. Steam power was not limited geographically
3. It was also not affected by weather

Core Skills
1. Chronology
2. Research
3. Empathy
4. Analysis

Drought

SOURCE 81
Yesterday was obliged to blow out ye new furnace our water being quite gone.
(Richard Ford, Coalbrookdale Ironworks)

Even at the Killhope Wheel (See 'Water Power'), with an annual rainfall of 63 inches, they were sometimes short of water in summer, or iced up in winter. The problem was especially acute in mines where water provided the power for pumping as a flooded mine could be severely damaged. Furthermore the demand for coal, tin, iron etc continued to grow. This meant mining deep and water powered pumps simply could not cope.

A step forward

Steam power had been around for centuries. Hero had used it for a curiosity at the University of Alexandria in the 1st century. Little had been heard of it since. However in 1690 Denis Papin in France produced a steam-atmospheric engine. In 1698 Thomas Savery invented a pump to draw water up mine shafts using steam and atmospheric pressure. It was not a steam engine and water wheels could be used to drive the same pumps. In 1712 Newcomen built an:

▶ What is a 'steam atmospheric' engine?

'ENGINE for Raising Water (with a power made) by FIRE'.

It too was a steam-atmospheric engine. Steam moved the piston up, atmospheric pressure moved the piston down when the steam had been condensed creating a vacuum. The Newcomen engine was large, clumsy, inefficient and expensive of fuel. It would only produce an up and down motion. Although it did make deeper mining possible it was not powerful enough to clear really deep mines. Its main advantage over the water wheel was that it worked throughout the year and was not affected by the weather. Improvements came fast—sometimes from unexpected quarters.

Newcomen's engine.

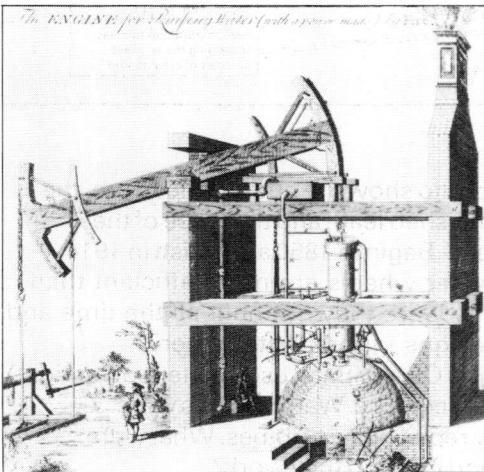

SOURCE 82
In the first fire-engines, a boy was constantly employed to open and shut alternately the communication between the boiler and the cylinder, according as the piston either ascended or descended. One of those boys, who loved to play with his companions, observed that, by tying a string from the handle of the valve which opened this communication to another part of the machine, the valve would open and shut without his assistance, and leave him at liberty to divert himself with his playfellows.
(Adam Smith, 'The Wealth of Nations', 1776)

SOURCE 83

On Friday last a steam engine was set to work at Bloomfield colliery, near Dudley. All the iron foundry parts were executed by Mr. Wilkinson; the condenser, with the valves, pistons and all the small work, at Soho. It made about 14 to 15 strokes per minute and emptied the engine-pit, which stood 57 feet deep in water, in less than an hour. This engine is applied to a pump which is capable of going to a depth of 300 feet with one fourth of the fuel that a common engine would require to produce the same quantity of power. The cylinder is 50 inches in diameter and the length of the stroke is 7 feet.
(*Birmingham Gazette,* 11th March 1776)

Steam power

▶ Why was the 'sun and planet' gear so called?

▶ What is rotary motion?

The real architect of the steam engine was James Watt. He took the Newcomen engine and improved it beyond measure:
1. The cylinder was closed, a valve box was added—steam now drove the piston in both directions.
2. Steam was condensed in a separate condenser—this prevented much waste of fuel by cooling the cylinder down at every stroke.
3. The 'sun and planet' gear gave rotary motion—this meant that steam engines could now be used for driving machines—invented with his foreman William Murdock.
4. Parallel motion was used to connect the piston to the beam—this kept the connecting rod vertical and helped to reduce loss of steam.
5. The centrifugal governor regulated the speed of the engine, keeping it steady—this was vital if it was to be used to drive machines.

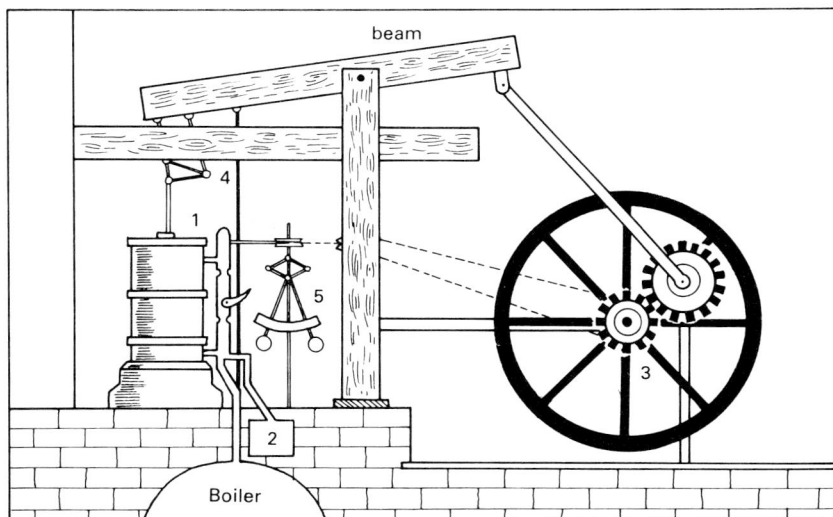

James Watt's engine.

SOURCE 84

Not till the invention of Watt's double-acting steam engine, was a prime mover found, that begot its own force by the consumption of coal and water, whose power was entirely under man's control, that was mobile and a means of locomotion, that was urban and not, like the water-wheel, rural, that permitted production to be concentrated in towns instead of, like the water wheels, being scattered up and down the country, that was of universal technical application, and, relatively speaking, little affected in its choice of residence by local circumstances.
(Karl Marx, 'Das Kapital', 1867)

A new age

The steam engine went everywhere, and into every industry.

SOURCE 85

In our populous towns a multitude of steam engines of all sizes, are continually at work for a great variety of purposes, such as pumping water, grinding corn, sawing timber and stone, rasping logwood, expressing oil from seeds, grinding cutlery, forming lead or copper into sheets or hollow pipes, fulling and scouring woollen cloth, twisting ropes and cables, drawing wire and for every description of laborious employment. We find them also in all extensive breweries and distilleries, in tanneries, soap manufactures, iron foundries and in the national establishments of dockyards and arsenals. Their number is daily increasing and they are continually applied to new purposes.
(John Farey, 'A Treatise on the Steam Engine', 1827)

There were said to be seventy five Newcomen engines at work in Cornish mines in 1777. By 1783 there was only one left. The advantages of the Boulton and Watt engine were obvious. Even so it is easy to exaggerate the impact of steam power. By 1800 there were probably only about 1250 steam engines in total, and of these some 300 were Newcomen engines. Not until 1850 was steam replacing water power on a large scale; steam engines in factories delivered only some 500 000 hp. Most firms were too small to afford an engine, or only had a small one. From 1850 onwards, however, the steam engine reigned supreme as the major source of power for industry.

SOURCE 86 — Boulton and Watt soon had competitors

The work belongs to Bateman and Sharrard, gentlemen every way qualified for so great an undertaking. Mr. Sharrard (cf Engineering) has improved upon and brought the steam engine to great perfection. Most of those used and set up about Manchester are of their make and setting up. They are in general of a small size, very compact, stand in a small space, work smooth and easy, and are scarcely heard in the building where erected. They are now used in cotton mills, and for every purpose of the water wheel, where a stream is not to be got, and for winding up coals from a great depth in the coal pits, which is performed with a quickness and ease not to be conceived.
(Sir F.M. Eden, 'The State of the Poor', 1797)

In 1835 the Milton Ironworks of Elsecar quoted for the supply of a steam engine to the Silkstone Colliery.

SOURCE 87

We now beg to hand you our terms for the Engine as requested; viz—high pressure with 13 in. Cylinder; Stroke of piston 3 feet, crosshead, guide rods, connecting rods, cranks and axle. Slide valve, eccentric motion with boiler of 6 sq. ft. of Horse Power, grate bars, fire doors and frame. All erected at Silkstone Common for £315:0:0

Watt's design was improved. Once the master patent ran out in 1800 those who advocated high pressure steam had their chance. Watt had stuck to low pressure steam, 5-10 lbs per sq. in., largely because he had doubts about existing boilers. The 'Cornish' engine began when Richard Trevithick adapted a Watt engine to run at a pressure of 40 lbs. for the Wheal Prosper mine. This was a large type of engine. Battersea pumping station had a 'Cornish' engine with a cylinder of 9 ft. 4 in. diameter.

▶ Why was high pressure so important for steam engines?

▶ Measure 9 ft 4 ins on the floor and see how big the cylinder of the Battersea pumping station was.

Boilers improved too with the development by Trevithick of the 'Cornish' boiler in 1812, and the 'Lancashire' boiler by William Fairbairn and John Hetherington of Manchester in 1844, which was more efficient still.

SOURCE 88 — Steam engines lasted a long time
There are many engines made by Boulton and Watt, forty years ago, which have been in constant work all that time with very slight repairs.
(A. Ure, 'The Philosophy of Manufacture', 1835)

An alternative to the huge 'Cornish' engines was to let high pressure steam expand partly in one cyclinder, then pass it to another cylinder to expand further. This is known as the compound engine, and it occupied less space. It was unsuccessful at first as steam pressures were not high enough for it to be worthwhile. Once pressures got to 100 lbs, however, it was highly successful. From about 1845 William McNaught of Manchester converted older Boulton and Watt type engines to compound action. It gave increased power for much less than the cost of a new engine. Three huge compound engines, built by Harveys of Hayle, in Cornwall, drained the Haarlem Mere for the Dutch, lifting 2.8 million tons of water per day.

Trevithick was responsible for a further development. For the Wheal Hope mine in Cornwall he built a small steam winding engine, known as a "puffer whim", which did not use a condenser but released high pressure steam into the atmosphere. No beam was needed. It was compact. It was portable. It was delivered to the mine in an ordinary farm cart for 10s 6d.

SOURCE 89
Steam-engines furnish the means not only of their support but of their multiplication. They create a vast demand for fuel; and, while they lend their powerful arms to drain the pits and raise the coals, they call into employment multitudes of miners, engineers, ship-builders and sailors, and cause the construction of canals and railways. Steam-engines moreover, by the cheapness and steadiness of their action, fabricate cheap goods, and procure in their exchange a liberal supply of the necessities and comforts of life.
(A. Ure, op. cit.)

▶ What were the advantages of the 'puffer whim' as a source of power?

▶ Why do you think the following were so called?
 a 'puffer whim' (The chapter on coal might help with the 'whim').
 a Cornish engine
 a Lancashire boiler

▶ List as many industries as you can that used steam engines.

Questions

1. Draw a time line to show the improvements in steam power up to 1850.
2. Can you arrange with your Science Department to see how hard you can blow? Can you blow as hard as the 5-10 psi used by Watt? As hard as the 40 psi used by Trevithick? As hard as the 100 psi used later? What to you think the letters psi stand for?
3. Why was steam power such an advantage over previous forms of power?
4. How many ways can you find in which the use of steam power would alter the lives of working people?
5. Write an obituary for your local newspaper for each of the following: Thomas Savery, Matthew Boulton, William Murdock.
6. You have been hired as a consulting engineer to advise on steam engines for a new cotton mill in 1855. Write a report saying what kind of steam engine and boiler you would recommend and why.

'Workshop of the World'

Key Ideas
1. The Great Exhibition
2. Britain in 1851
3. Trade
4. Relation of industry to transport

Core Skills
1. Comprehension
2. Statistical
3. Analysis
4. Synthesis

The Great Exhibition 1851

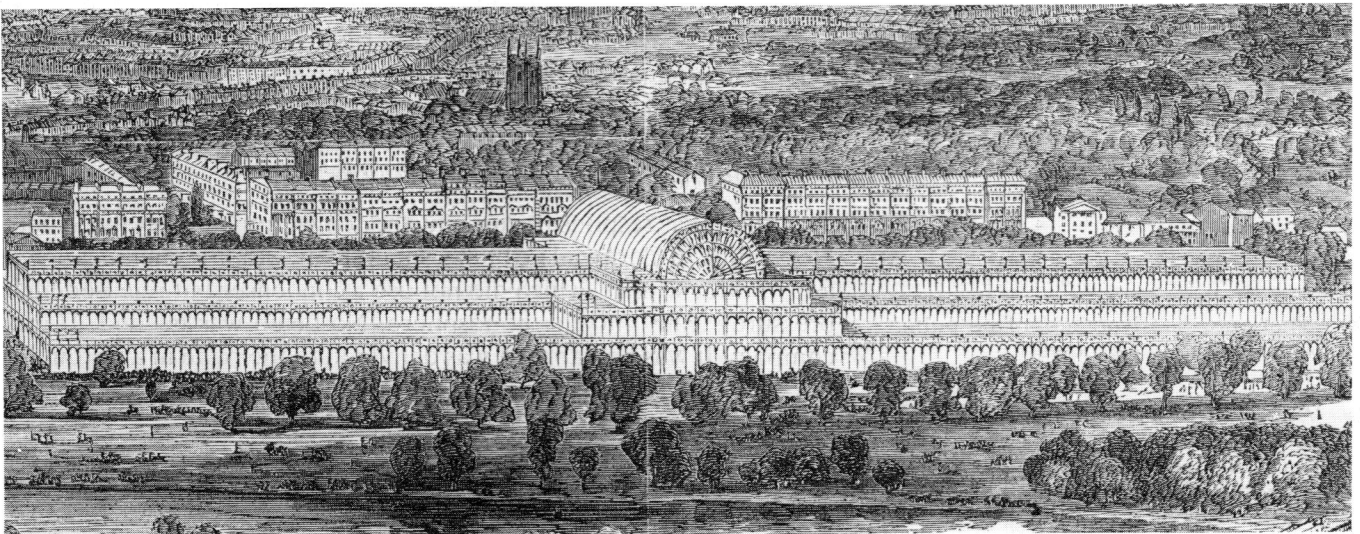

The Crystal Palace, built to house the Great Exhibition.

THE POUND AND THE SHILLING.
"Whoever Thought of Meeting You Here?"

Everyone went to the Great Exhibition.

SOURCE 90
'God bless my dear country which has shown itself so great today' (Queen Victoria, 1st May 1851)

The Great Exhibition held in the 'Crystal Palace' in Hyde Park was an international exhibition in that it had exhibits from countries in all parts of the world. In fact it was intended to show off British industrial prowess to the world, and the manufacturing sections were dominated by Britain. The very building in which it was held was a showpiece for the new British industry. The iron frames were prefabricated and put together using the same techniques that railway engineers used to build iron bridges. The glass was a product of an industry that had only learned to make sheet glass in 1832. The exhibition was a triumph. It proved to the British that their country was the 'Workshop of the World'.

SOURCE 91
Perhaps the best way of realizing the progress of the last half-century would be to fancy ourselves suddenly transferred to the year 1800, with all our habits, expectations, requirements, and standard of living formed upon the luxuries and appliances collected round us in 1850.

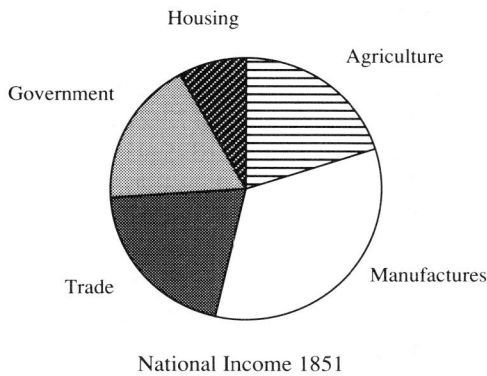

National Income 1851

In the first year of the century we should find ourselves eating bread at 1s 10½d the quartern loaf. We should find ourselves grumbling at heavy taxes laid on nearly all the necessaries and luxuries of life receiving our newspapers seldom and some days after date; receiving our Edinburgh letters in London a week after they were written, and paying thirteen pence halfpenny for them to be delivered; exchanging the instantaneous telegraph for the slow and costly express by chaise and pair; travelling with soreness and fatigue by the 'old heavy' (coach) at the rate of seven miles an hour, instead of by the Great Western (railway) at fifty; and relapsing from the blaze of light which gas now pours along our streets, into a perilous and uncomfortable darkness made visible by a few wretched oil lamps scattered at distant intervals.
(*The Economist*, 1851)

Britain in 1851 had undergone what we today would term an 'industrial revolution', but she was not the country that we see around us today. It is clear from the list of major occupations given below how true this was. Most companies were very small, many depending largely on skilled craftsmen. Mass production tended to be happening in only a few major industries—coal, iron and cotton especially. The great move to factory production was yet to come, helped by the development of new industries which went into factory production from the beginning.

Occupations

The ten most common occupations in 1851 were:

Farming	1 790 000
Domestic service	1 039 000
Textiles (cotton, silk, linen)	527 000
Building work	443 000
Labouring	376 000
Sewing	340 000
Wool	284 000
Shoemaking	274 000
Coalmining	219 000
Tailoring	143 000

▶ Which occupations would not be in the 'top ten' today?

Population

The population of England and Wales since 1700 was (in millions):

1701	5.8	1781	7.5
1711	6.0	1791	8.3
1721	6.0	1801	9.2
1731	6.1	1811	10.2
1741	6.2	1821	12.0
1751	6.5	1831	13.9
1761	6.7	1841	15.9
1771	7.2	1851	17.9

Growth of towns

	1801	1851
Birmingham	73 670	232 841
Bristol	63 645	137 238
Leeds	53 162	172 270
Liverpool	77 653	375 955
London	818 129	2 133 202
Manchester	84 020	316 213
Norwich	36 832	68 195
Newcastle	28 366	87 784
Sheffield	31 314	135 310
Cardiff	1 870	8 065
Swansea	6 099	16 249
Glasgow	77 385	329 097
Edinburgh	82 560	160 302

▶ Match the towns listed with those marked on the map 'Great Britain 1850' on page 74.

Index of industrial production

1800	23.06
1811	29.03
1821	37.6
1831	52.4
1841	72.9
1851	100

(1851 = 100)

Index of average wages

1800	95
1810	124
1820	110
1831	101
1841	100
1850	100

(1850 = 100)

Coal

In 1700 there were 205 chauldrons (53 cwts) of coal shipped from Newcastle to London. By 1832 the figure had risen to 1 211 chauldrons.

Tynemouth Dock, Newcastle, 1910.

▶ Work out how many tons of coal were shipped from Newcastle to London in 1700 and 1832? What would the figure be in kilograms?

Metal

In 1720 the production of pig iron was 25 000 tons. By 1852 production had risen to 2 701 000 tons.

There are no figures available for the early eighteenth century but production of metallic ores (tons) in the mid-nineteenth century was:

Tin	9 455	(1851)
Copper	184.9	(1854)
Lead	102.0	(1851)

► What changes had made the massive increase in the production of pig iron possible?

Textiles

The largest industry in the country was textiles. Things were changing here also:

Date	Factory Workers	Handloom Weavers
1806	90 000	184 000
1811	102 000	204 000
1821	129 000	240 000
1831	187 000	240 000
1841	264 000	110 000
1851	339 000	40 000

In 1851, the means and source of power for textile production could be broken down as follows:

	Cotton	Wool	Silk	Linen & other
	(Numbers are in thousands)			
Spindles	20 977	2 471	1 226	965
Power looms	250	42	6	4
Horse power				
steam	46	23	3	11
water	12	10	1	3

SOURCE 92 — The effects of mining on the countryside

The Black Country is anything but picturesque. The earth seems to have been torn inside out. Its entrails are strewn about; nearly the entire surface of the ground is covered with cinder-heaps. The coal, which has been drawn from below ground, is blazing on the surface. The district is crowded with iron furnaces, puddling furnaces and coal-pit engine furnaces. By day and night the country is glowing with fire. There is a rumbling and clanking of iron forges and rolling mills.
(James Nasmyth, 1850s)

Trade

SOURCE 93

'The silk of China is woven in Coventry and sold wholesale in New York, retailed in New Orleans and consumed by a neighbouring planter's wife as a ribbon attached to her dress. The American planter grows cotton wool which is exported and woven into cloth in Manchester. This cloth finds its way into the interior of Bengal, and may be paid for in produce which will be sold for food in the English market ten thousand miles off. A halfpennyworth of meal from America, a halfpennyworth of coffee from Jamaica, a halfpennyworth of sugar from Brazil are sold at this same humble counter to the occupant of a neighbouring garret in St. Giles. A chandler's shop in the dirtiest, darkest thoroughfare of the outskirts of London or Limerick cannot exist without supplies from every quarter of the globe.'
(Felkin, 'The Exhibition of 1851 of the Products and Industry of all Nations: Its probable influence upon Labour and Commerce')

► Match the numbered towns with those listed in the table at the top of p. 72.

Great Britain in 1850.

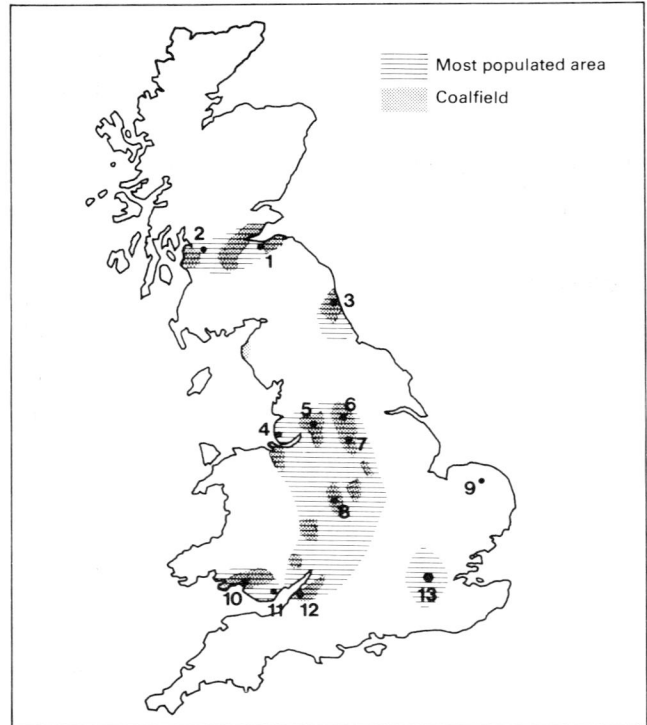

Most populated area

Coalfield

Railways in Britain, 1850.

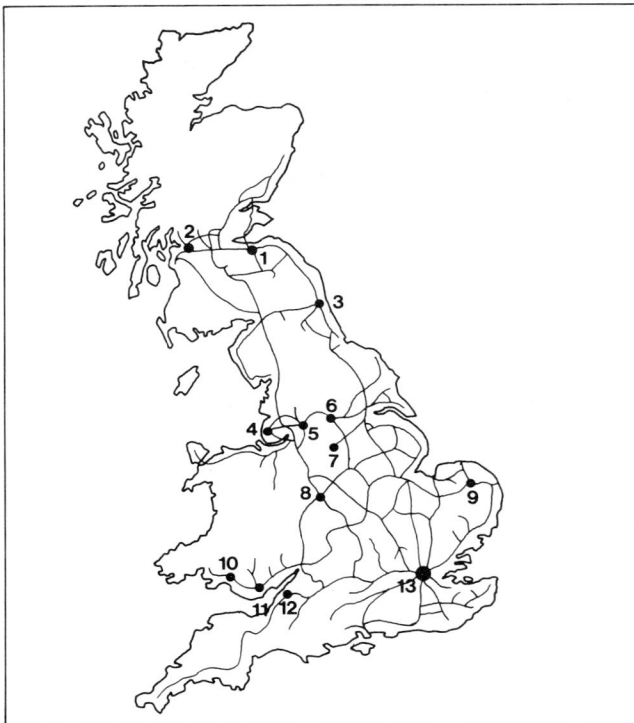

Canals in Britain, 1850.

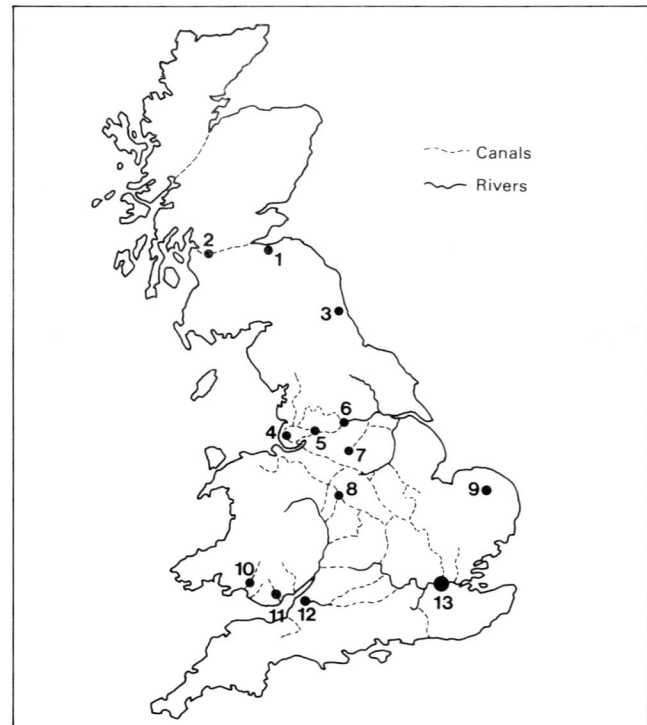

Canals

Rivers

► List all the countries you can find that traded with Britain.
► What were the advantages of the railway as a means of transport?
► What were the other main means of transport in 1851?

SOURCE 94

The practice of employing children only six or seven years of age is all but universal . . . The children go down the pit with the men usually at four o'clock in the morning, and remain in the pit between eleven and twelve hours each day.
(Children's Employment Commission, Report on the Mines, 1842)

SOURCE 95

At what time in the morning, in the brisk time, did these girls go to the mills?
    In the brisk time, for about six weeks, they have gone at 3 o'clock in the morning, and ended at ten, or nearly half-past, at night.*

What intervals were allowed for rest or refreshment?
    Breakfast, quarter of an hour, and dinner half an hour, and drinking quarter of an hour.

*Normal hours were 6 am to 8.30 p.m.
(Report on Factory Children's Labour, 1831-2)

▶ How many hours did the mill-girls work:
a. In the busy time?
b. Normally?
If they were paid 15p per week normally and 3p extra during the busy period, how much did they earn each day? Can you work out an hourly rate?

SOURCE 96

One of the most prominent social characteristics of the present time is the growth and progress of pleasure travelling among the people. The working classes of thirty, or even fifteen years ago, did not know their own country. Very few travelled for pleasure beyond a small circle around the places which they inhabited. But now industrious men of the Midland Counties, whose forefathers never saw the sea, are enabled to gain physical as well as mental enjoyment by a view of its mighty waters. Already the working classes have commenced laying by their weekly pence to form a fund for visiting London during the Great Exhibition of 1851.
(*Illustrative London News*, 21st September 1850)

The Great Exhibition was opened on 1st May, 1851 in the Crystal Palace in Hyde Park. It was open for a mere 141 days and in that time was visited by more than 6 000 000 people. About 13 000 exhibitors, roughly half from Britain or the Empire, the rest foreign, showed goods of all sorts.

SOURCE 97

There was yesterday witnessed a sight the like of which has never happened before.

. . . We do not see why every child whom its parents can bring up to town should not take lessons at the Exhibition. But . . . it is not uncommon to find grown up people as ill informed as their own children. All ages therefore will find it to their advantage to go to school for the season in Hyde Park.
(*The Times*, 2nd May 1851)

A model of a steam engine, an exhibit at the Great Exhibition.

▶ Why do you think that the 'Times' felt all children should go to the Great Exhibition?

Questions

1. In what ways did Britain change between 1700 and 1851?
2. Do you think people were better or worse off in 1851 than they had been in 1700? Explain your answer.
3. In what ways is Britain today different from the Britain of 1851? What changes were still to come?

'The Great Depression'

Key Ideas
1. Decline of staple industries
2. Not really a depression—except in agriculture
3. Impact of development in other countries

Core Skills
1. Comprehension of evidence
2. Use of Graphs and Statistics
3. Inferring from evidence
4. Making judgements based on evidence

A cloud

There were developments, small at the time but 'Continental talented men might take part of the business of this country' (Presidential Address to the Institution of Mechanical Engineers, George Stephenson, 1847).

Robbins & Lawrence exhibited at the Great Exhibition rifles so accurately machined that their parts were interchangeable.

Foreign apprentices received their training in British engineering shops—eg the brothers Krupp, and so was founded the core of Germany's industrial prowess.

British engineers emigrated, taking their skills with them—eg Charles Brown, trained at Maudslay, Sons and Field, went to Switzerland, played a key part in developing Sulzers and founded the Swiss Locomotive Co. His sons founded Brown Boveri & Co. A major part of Swiss heavy engineering was in existence. Crompton and Slater went to the United States and founded the textile industry in New England, and the engineering that went with it.

Trade

In 1865 and 1871 two significant things happened for British trade. In 1865 the American Civil War came to an end. In 1871 the new state of Germany was formed. America could concentrate on industrial production, helped by the huge numbers of European immigrants. Corn and beef began to flow from the prairies of the American West to the Eastern states and later to Europe. Germany too, united as a single nation for the first time, was able to develop her industry.

Argentina was developing, largely with British finance. She began to produce cattle on a large scale. Two new technological developments were important. As early as 1665 iron sheets were coated with tin. By the 1870s this had become steel sheets and the result was being used to produce tin cans in which food could be preserved. Refrigeration was invented during the 1870s by Karl von Linde in Germany. These inventions, coupled with the use of the steamship meant that meat could be sent from Argentina to the markets of Europe, in particular to Britain. Australia was being opened up and producing identical products.

SOURCE 98 — Britain faced agricultural problems
There is agreement as to the extent of the distress which has fallen upon the agricultural community. Owners and occupiers have alike suffered from it. All without distinction have been involved in a general calamity.
('Report from H.M. Commissioners on Agriculture', 1882)

Rainfall patterns

1854-74 Average rainfall	26.5	ins per annum
1875	34	ins
1876	34.5	ins
1877	33.5	ins
1878	32.3	ins
1879	36	ins
1880	34	ins

▶ Work out the average rainfall for the years 1875-80.

▶ What effect would this rainfall have on wheat farmers?

▶ What effect would this rainfall have on beef farmers?

▶ What would you expect to happen to the price of wheat during this period? And why?

▶ Why then is the price of wheat falling consistently during this period (See Source 99)?

Agricultural selling prices

From 1877 to 1897 the price fell by:

Wheat	50%
Beef	40%
Wool	50%
Potatoes	40%

Successive governments, obsessed with Free Trade would not give protection.

Punch cartoon, 1896, 'Caught Napping'.
The caption was
'There was an old lady as I've heard tell,
She went to market her goods for the sell,
She went to market on a market day
And she fell asleep on the world's highway.
By came a pedlar — German — and stout,
And he cut her petticoats all round about.'

SOURCE 99 — Mr J.B. Lawes was called in and examined

I would ask you whether the agricultural depression of the last few years has affected you to any extent?
In common with other farmers it certainly has.

In what respect?
By the very bad crops I have had, and the great injury done to my land by the wet, and by the growth of weeds.

What do you consider to have been the primary cause of the depression?
The excessive wet and the low prices.

How many years do you consider the agricultural depression has lasted?
Six years I consider it to be.
('Royal Commission on Agriculture, minutes of evidence', 1881)

▶ Was Mr Lawes (Source 99) right or wrong about the rainfall? Explain your answer.

SOURCE 100 — America's grain production, 1879

In the cereal year ending August 1879, wheat production in America first astonished Europe; in 1880 increased exports were partly attributed to extraordinary efforts made to substitute the great European crop deficiencies from the bad harvest of 1879; but the present season shows the clear truth that the wheat the United States will produce must entirely change the general situation of the wheat trade.

(*The Economist*, 12th March 1881)

SOURCE 101 — Exports

Let us admit that our exports, as measured in nominal values, considerably diminished since those roaring years of prosperity, 1872 and 1873. They were £256 and £255 millions in those years, and £191 and £223 millions in 1879 and 1880. In 1882 they were £241 millions and in 1884 £233 millions, further decreasing to £213 millions in 1885. Let us admit, too, that this decrease of exports has been the sign and result of a real depression, and that both profits and wages have decreased since those so-called prosperous years.

(Sir Thomas H. Farrer, Cobden Club, 'Free trade versus fair trade', 1886)

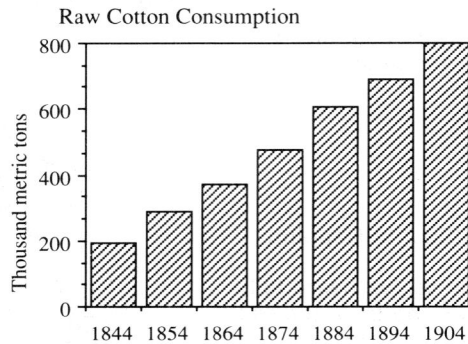

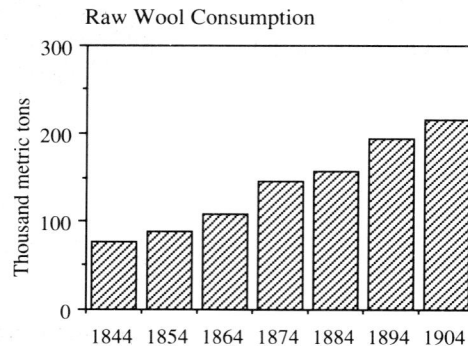

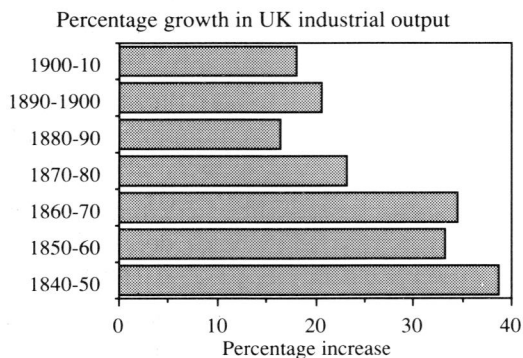

Raw Cotton Consumption

Raw Wool Consumption

Percentage growth in UK industrial output

Production and Income

	Total Industrial Production (as % of 1913 production)	National Income per head* (at 1913 prices)
1865	44.7	23.98
1866	46.1	24.27
1867	47.5	23.89
1868	49.0	23.76
1869	50.5	24.86
1870	52.0	26.84
1871	53.4	27.54
1872	54.8	27.11
1873	56.2	28.81
1874	57.5	30.29
1875	58.8	29.77
1876	60.0	29.82
1877	61.1	29.67
1878	62.0	30.45
1879	63.0	29.56
1880	64.0	29.68
1881	64.9	31.38
1882	65.9	32.33
1883	66.7	33.24
1884	67.5	33.65
1885	68.4	34.69

*National Income is the amount that the country earned in the year

▶ Draw a graph for each of these sets of figures, Industrial Production and National Income.

▶ During the period 1875-1885 what happens to:
   a. Industrial Production?
   b. National Income?

▶ Are there any significant changes to the general trend during this period?

Prices at which goods could be sold on the world's markets had gone down:

	Prices (per ton)	
	1874	1883
steel rails	£12 0s 0d	£5 7s 6d
iron rails	£ 9 18s 0d	£5 0s 0d
pig iron	£ 4 17 6d	£1 13s 0d

SOURCE 102 — Prices of raw materials had gone up
For example, during 1879 the wholesale prices in London have undergone these elevations, viz, Manilla hemp, 62 per cent; Scotch pig iron, 50; British bars, 35; tin 38; raw cotton, 37; cotton yarn, 26; tea, 36; lead, 31; jute, 27; tallow, 25; sugar, 21; silk, 19; flax, 18; wheat, 18; copper, 13; coffee, 13; wool, 9 per cent . . .
(*The Economist,* 12th March 1881)

Freight Charges — Chicago to Liverpool (per ton)

1868	£3 5s 0d
1882	£1 4s 0d

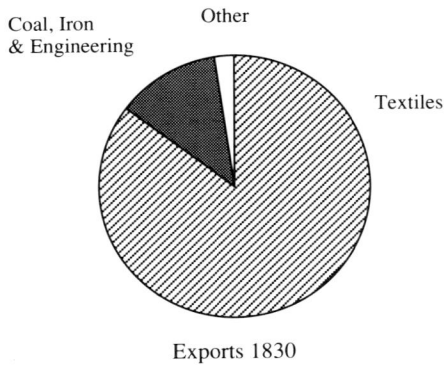

Exports 1830

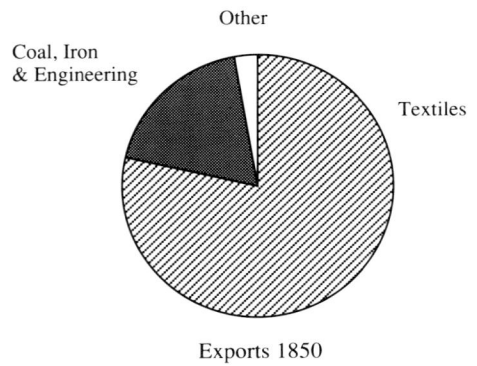

Exports 1850

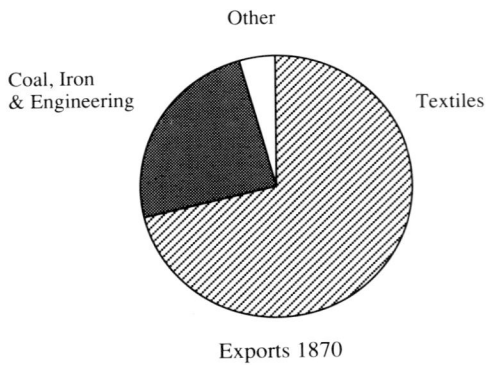

Exports 1870

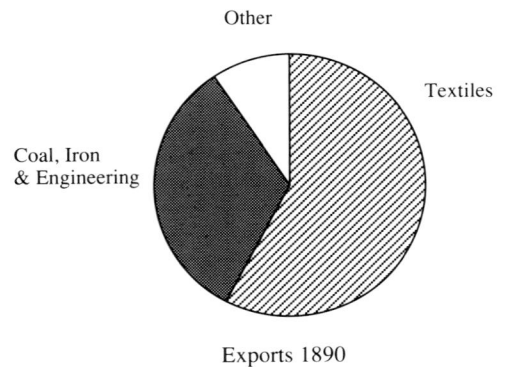

Exports 1890

▶ Which sector of industry was declining in importance?

▶ Which sector of industry was increasing in importance?

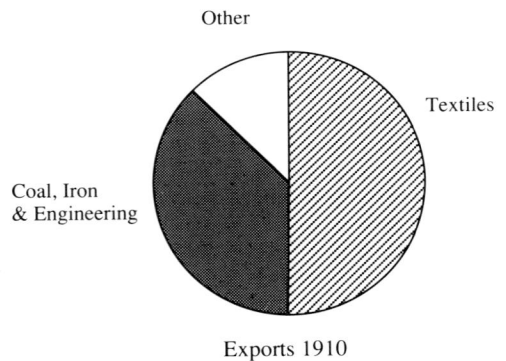

Exports 1910

Questions

1. What do we understand by the term 'depression'?
2. Do you think there was a depression in agriculture during the late 1870s? Explain your answer fully.
3. What were the causes of the agricultural depression?
4. During this period, what happened to:
   a. Prices of raw materials?
   b. Selling prices of finished goods?
   c. Profits?

5. On the basis of the sources available, how far do you think it was true to say that Britain suffered a 'great depression'.

A New World

Key Ideas
1. New industries—gas, electricity
2. New uses for old products—tinplate, galvanised iron
3. New forms of transport
4. Service industries—eg garages
5. Opportunities missed—chemicals and electricals

Core Skills
1. Asking Historical Questions
2. Use of evidence
3. Synthesis

New industries

The Industrial Revolution did not really alter the manufacturing base of the country. Coal, iron and textiles provided a good living for 150 years, and change occurred mainly within these areas. The situation was changing, Germany and the USA were both overtaking Britain.

SOURCE 103

Manufacturers in this country do not lay down large capacity plants, as are common in the United States and Germany.

The combination of up-to-date plants, economies, and improvements has enabled our American rivals, paying the highest wages known in the trade, to produce plates at a cost of only about 3s 6d per ton for labour, averaging some 225 tons of plates per shift. These results are not equalled in our own mills.
(Report of the Tariff Commission, 1904)

▶ How was the USA, with high wages, able to sell goods cheaper than Britain?

Things did not seem too bad, however. New industries like chemicals and electricity were expanding rapidly. Once more Britain was prosperous and expanding. All was well! Or was it? The flow of machinery into and out of the United Kingdom might have given pause for thought.

Machinery and mill work 1897-1907

	Imports	Exports
Steam Engines—		
Locomotive	64%	191%
Agricultural	88%	44%
Other	83%	72%
Non steam engines—		
Agricultural	94%	33%
Sewing machines	29%	119%
Mining machinery	200%	19%
Textile machinery	93%	3%
Other—		
including electrical machinery	10%	116%

- ▶ Which industries formed the main base of British industry?

- ▶ In what kinds of machinery was Britain not doing so well?

- ▶ In what kinds of machinery was Britain doing well?

- ▶ What are the characteristics of modern industry shown by cycle manufacture?

The British were doing well at what they had been doing for the last hundred years, in particular steam engineering. They saw no reason to change however, and there were new forms of power about. The internal combustion engine that drives our cars and lorries was being developed by German and French engineers. The British, with few exceptions, felt that 'there was nothing like steam'. When internal combustion engines were used they were largely of German design.

Two key inventions were responsible for the development of the bicycle, the wire spoke tension wheel by Cowper in 1868 and the pneumatic tyre by Dunlop in 1888. The manufacture of bicycles flourished in Coventry. It showed many of the characteristics of modern industry.

SOURCE 104
Traders testify to the increasing specialisation of the industry. Considerable plant is necessary and the large investment of fixed capital would not be profitable unless the firm can ensure a large and fairly constant output.
(Carter, 'The Cycle Industry' in Seasonal Trades, 1912)

The cycle industry, coupled with the internal combustion engine led to the motor car and motor-cycle.

SOURCE 105
THE MOTORING INDUSTRY
AN ENORMOUS ANNUAL EXPENDITURE
GROWTH OF EMPLOYMENT

It has been estimated that on January 1 over 440 000 motors of all kinds were in use in the British Isles. Nearly 1 700 additional vehicles are being added to this total every week. Motoring has been the means of building up a vast industry.
(*The Times*, 3rd February 1914)

A telephone exchange in the 1900s.

Cars in those days were started by turning a handle at the front. When an American engineer tried to sell a self-starter to a British car firm he was told it would cost £20-£50 per car, and 'our' owners have chauffeurs. The Americans produced in quantity for a mass market.

SOURCE 106 — Factory inspectors noted developments in southern England
Electric power has taken the place of gas and steam in a good many factories.

The two principal developments are the laying down of a large number of gas producing plants in factories . . . and the introduction of electric motor driven machinery . . .

Many small occupiers have gone in for power, thus converting their workshops into factories.

The erection of three important generating stations in West London, including one which will be the largest in the kingdom.

The development of the motor-car industry has called into being an ever-increasing number of 'garages' in the West of London, the majority of which are fitted with a repairing plant driven by power . . .

Transport was changed — a tram.

► Find out what 'galvanising' is.

► What is a by-product?

► What does a refinery do?

► Why would Avonmouth docks be a good site for a refinery?

Roberts Dale & Co. Chemical Works, Lancashire, after an explosion in 1887.

A few of the country factories now rely almost entirely on motor wagons for the carriage of their manufactures to their warehouses in London.
('Annual Report of Factory Inspectors', 1905)

SOURCE 107
It is questionable if any large electrical factories have made real profit in the last two years. Even the best British factories are hardly equal in size and equipment to leading works in Germany, whose competition is felt for export orders.
(*The Economist*, 16th February 1907)

SOURCE 108
In particular some of the metal trades have experienced another year's prosperity and growth. Extension of old works, better equipment and speeding up of plant, and the erection of new concerns in the steel, sheet and tinplate trades have marked the year's activities in South Wales and Monmouthshire. In the Swansea district Mr. Hilditch refers to a large plant in the course of erection at a copper works for the extraction of precious metals by electrolysis. Mr. Edwards (Cardiff) records extensive additions at a leading sheet rolling plant at Newport for the galvanising trade. Not the least interesting feature of the coke and chemical industries is the installation of by-product ovens . . . The patent fuel (Coal briquettes) trade of South Wales shows considerable expansion. A scheme is afoot for the erection of a large refinery at Avonmouth Docks. He also records that the recently established aeroplane factory at Filton has the reputation of being the 'largest purely aeroplane works in the world'.
('Annual Report of Factory Inspectors', 1911)

SOURCE 109
Two industries commenced during the past year. In one case British aluminium is produced. In the other case, carbide of calcium—the source of the new illuminant acetylene gas—is manufactured by the electric arc.
('Annual Report of Factory Inspectors', 1896)

The chemical industry developed in a piecemeal way. The Gilchrist-Thomas method of lining steel furnaces with limestone gave waste that could be used as a fertiliser. This was perhaps the first example of a by-product. In 1785 Berthollet discovered that chlorine could be used to bleach cloth. Tennants of Glasgow were bleaching with chloride of lime from 1797. Within 25 years they had the biggest chemical works in Europe. Soda, industry's most important alkali, was used in the manufacture of soap and glass. A major raw material was salt and small firms were established, in the mid-Mersey valley, on the great Cheshire salt field. A second material used in the production of soda was sulphuric acid, industry's most important acid. In the production of this other by-products resulted. A fourth strand was the discovery of a method of extracting a purple dye from coal tar by William Perkin in 1856 which led to a whole range of aniline dyes.

► Why should you not be surprised to find a large glass factory at St. Helens, near the Mersey valley?

The chemical industry was successful but it still lagged behind that of Germany.

Questions

1. Explain, in as much detail as you can, why other countries were developing their industries faster than Britain by the end of the nineteenth century.
2. What difference did the increasing use of electricity as a source of power make to industry? (Location of industry, pollution, getting power to different parts of the factory, convenience, safety, impact on other industries are some of the points you might consider).
3. Some new industries had affected existing industries and caused new industries to be started. How would you expect the development of motor vehicles to affect other industries?
4. What differences would you expect the development of motor vehicles to make to the lives of people. (Remember only the very rich would have a car before the First World War).

Depression

Key Ideas
1. The decline of staple industries especially in north
2. The growth of new industries
3. The Wall Street Crash
4. International nature of the problem
5. Not a universal problem—the dichotomy between employed and unemployed

Core Skills
1. Statistics
2. Asking historical questions
3. Historical Ideas
4. Analysis

War

Wars are good for industry, if not for people. There is a huge demand for all kinds of goods, profits for the firms that sell them, jobs for the men and women that produce them. The Great War, 1914-1918, was no exception. After the war there was a boom period as industry made all the consumer goods which people had wanted that had not been available during the war.

SOURCE 110—Problems created by war
The shortage (and higher prices) which developed as factories changed over to war production encouraged other countries to manufacture for themselves goods which they had previously brought in Britain, and gave competitors an advantage which they were not slow to seize. The United States took over British markets in South America and the Japanese moved into Britain's most important market, India.
(G. Turner, 'Business in Britain', Spottiswoode, 1969)

The true situation, undistorted by war, was beginning to show itself. Even before the Great War there were suggestions that the situation for Britain was changing.

SOURCE 111
Methods of production first established in the United Kingdom, have since 1870 extended to foreign countries . . . from which British products have been shut out by import duties.

English engineers visiting America have been surprised to see so few men about. Automatic machinery is much more largely used.
('Report of the Tariff Commission', 1904)

SOURCE 112
Between 1913 and 1921, according to one estimate, the total output of US manufacturing industry rose by twenty-two per cent, that of Japan by seventy-six per cent; Britain's output, on the other hand, actually fell—by 7½ per cent.
(G. Turner, op. cit.)

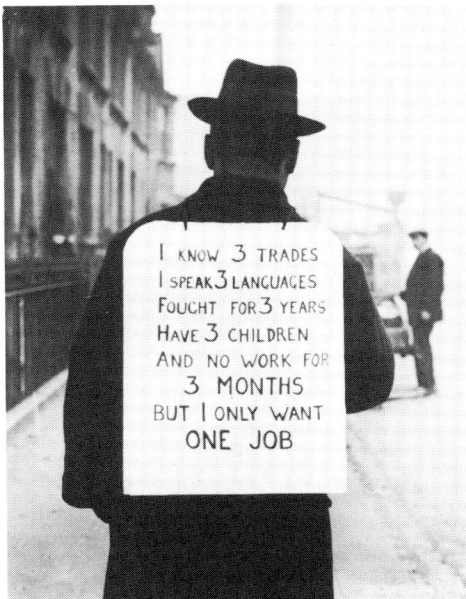
An unemployed man.

I KNOW 3 TRADES
I SPEAK 3 LANGUAGES
FOUGHT FOR 3 YEARS
HAVE 3 CHILDREN
AND NO WORK FOR
3 MONTHS
BUT I ONLY WANT
ONE JOB

▶ Why did the state of British industry not become clear before 1922?

With the war over, the post-war boom beginning to peter out, the predicament became clearer.

SOURCE 113 — Coal

The very perfection of the textile and other machinery by which Britain won her industrial leadership has enabled it to be worked fairly well by backward races. Little more than mere order and organised discipline will go a long way towards success, where the same tasks are performed by modern machinery, which does most of the thinking itself. Consequently England will not be able to hold her own against other nations by mere practice of familiar processes.
('Official Papers by Alfred Marshall', Ed. J.M. Keynes, 1926)

SOURCE 114 — Steel

. . . ever since the armistice, the great basic exporting industries— coal, metallurgy, and textiles—have been in a bad way.

There is not a general trade depression. New industries have sprung up, or have grown from small beginnings, which have provided compensation for the decline in the basic trades. Meanwhile there has been steady expansion in a great variety of miscellaneous occupations, catering mainly for the home market.
('Britain's industrial future', a Liberal Party Yellow Book, 1928)

▶ In what ways was British industry lagging behind our competitors from other countries? (Hint: It would be helpful to refer to the previous chapter.)

▶ What new industries were 'springing up' or 'growing from small beginnings'?

▶ What do you think Marshall means by the 'mere practice of familiar processes'?

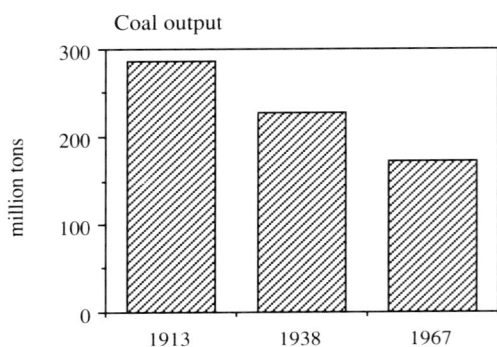

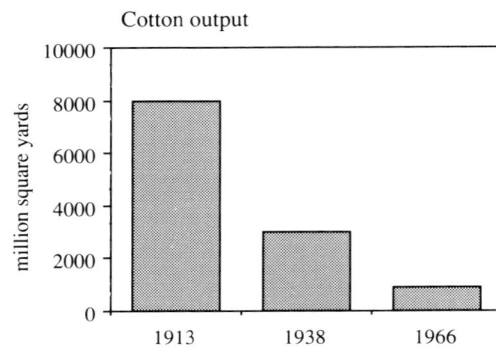

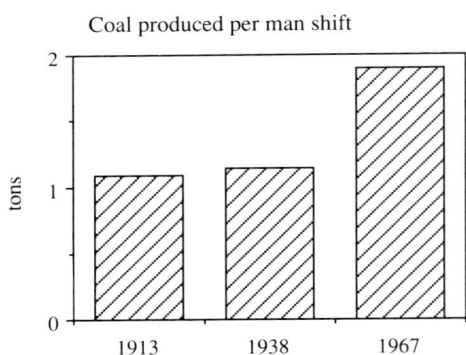

Coal output

million tons

300 / 1913
200 / 1938
~175 / 1967

Cotton output

million square yards

8000 / 1913
3000 / 1938
~900 / 1966

Coal produced per man shift

tons

~1.1 / 1913
~1.15 / 1938
~1.9 / 1967

Britain was facing problems in the traditional trades which had made her rich. The situation was to get worse. There were huge falls in the prices of stocks and shares on the American Stock Market in 1929. This was known as the Wall Street Crash. This in turn set off a 'chain reaction' in other stock markets through the world. It illustrated quite clearly that trade and finance was an international business and that what happened in one country affected all the others. It also caused trade throughout the world to slow down. Nobody could afford to buy—so little was sold, and many manufacturers went bankrupt, causing huge unemployment.

SOURCE 115 — Effects of the Wall Street Crash

The sight was one of the most doleful I have ever seen. It consisted chiefly of this: Men standing with their hands in their pockets along the street kerb. If I asked some of them, they would tell me they were 'waiting for something to pass by'—a chance to run an errand, or do something for a few pence.
(*The Sphere*, 28th February 1931)

▶ What was the 'Wall Street Crash'?

▶ Could a similar thing happen again today?

Only the most modern factories, which could produce their goods at the lowest possible cost survived. With little international trade fewer ships were needed. Shipbuilding was particularly badly hit.

THE SKELETON AT THE FEAST.
A TABLEAU OMITTED FROM TO-DAY'S LORD MAYOR'S SHOW.

Punch cartoon, 1932, commenting on British agriculture.

Now there was a general depression, but even so most of what the Liberal party had said in 1928 held good. It was the basic trades that were hit hardest. Newer industries were still developing. Electrical equipment began to be manufactured on a large scale as electricity was put into most houses, and was used to light our streets. As early as 1930 no less than 66% of industrial power came from electricity, and of the major factory trades only textiles gained less than half their power from electricity.

The rubber industry grew greatly between the wars, as did the oil industry. In both cases the impact of motor vehicles is clear. The production of cars shot up with the adoption of American assembly-line methods. Motor cycle manufacture boomed in the 1920s and fell away in the 1930s. Light vans used the same mass-production methods as cars and output expanded rapidly. Heavy lorries, using the diesel engine, were still made by hand but added to output and employment.

Two of our most important industries, although developing significantly, were not to make their major impact until after the Second World War. The aircraft industry, after a boom in the Great War, really began to grow as metal-skinned monoplanes with better engines and more sophisticated propellers came in the 1930s. Rearmament during this period helped. The chemical industry was expanding with many new products including fertilisers, medicines and cosmetics. Even so it was providing only 2.1% of Britain's national income in 1935, having given 1.1% in 1907. A completely new material came from the chemical industry as the first plastics were developed. Bakelite was used to make plugs and electrical fittings. Rayon was the first man-made fibre. As in the case of motor vehicles the cost of equipment was high and mergers and take-overs led to fewer but larger companies such as ICI.

The British Broadcasting Company (later to become the British Broadcasting Corporation) was set up in 1922. There was a high demand for the new radio sets. The problem was that all the other advanced nations were making all these things too, often cheaper than Britain was.

There were many new occupations connected with the cinema, radio, and cars, for example. Many of these new occupations were concerned with doing things for people rather than making things, and mostly for people in Britain. International trade was badly hit.

In the north, where most of the basic industries had been, unemployment was 30-40 per cent. In the south, where most of the new 'light' industries were, it was down to 6 per cent. The result was that the majority of the population became better off, even at this time.

▶ What do you think is meant by the term 'service industry'?

▶ Why do you think so many of the new industries are referred to as 'light industries'?

▶ What would you class as 'heavy industry'?

Questions

1. What caused unemployment in Britain in the 1930s?
2. How far is it true to say that Britain suffered from her own success? (Remember what was in the earlier chapter as well as what you have read in this one.)
3. If incomes per head were still going up in the 1930s, what signs were there that British industry was not in the good position that it had once held?
4. Why do you think that Britain's industrial competitors were doing better than Britain in the inter-war period?

The Old Economics

Key Ideas
1. Colonies
2. Protection
3. Laissez-Faire
4. The Corn Laws

Core Skills
1. Comprehension
2. Research

SOURCE 116 — Smuggling
Running round the woodlump
    if you should chance to find
Little barrels, roped and tarred,
    all full of brandy-wine;
Don't you shout to come and look,
    nor take 'em for your play;
Put the brushwood back again,
    —and they'll be gone next day!
('A Smugglers' Song', Rudyard Kipling)

Laissez-Faire

Until the middle of the nineteenth century people believed that the government had only two functions:

a. To keep law and order at home,
b. To look after our relationships with other countries.

This policy was one of 'leave things alone', 'don't interfere', 'let sleeping dogs lie'. At least that was the idea, but putting it into practice was not always easy—and in any case it got mixed up with other ideas.

Colonies

► Which were the most important British colonies at that time?

► When, exactly, were the Navigation Acts passed?

Since Tudor times Britain had been acquiring colonies overseas gradually. Legally these were part of Britain, even if they were thousands of miles away. The Navigation Acts—really a series of Acts passed in the 1660s—said that all trade with British colonies should be carried out by Britain. Thus Britain would benefit from having these colonies rather than other countries benefitting. If countries wished to buy goods from British colonies they would buy them from Britain. Britain was becoming rich.

Protection

There were relatively few modern taxes and one of the few ways of raising money for government was by customs duties placed on goods coming into Britain from abroad. There were other advantages too in that people would buy goods made in Britain rather than abroad. They would be cheaper as there were no customs duties to pay. British industry would be protected from foreign competition.

However this encouraged smuggling and by the late eighteenth and early nineteenth century it had become almost a national pastime. Even during the wars with France between 1793 and 1815 smuggling between the two countries continued.

SOURCE 117 — Ideas were beginning to change
To found a great empire for the sole purpose of raising up a people of customers is extremely fit for a nation that is governed by shopkeepers.
(Adam Smith, 'The Wealth of Nations', 1776)

Adam Smith went on to argue that shopkeepers earn their living buying and selling, and as a trading nation Britain should do the same. Customs duties discouraged people from trading. Customs duties should be reduced as they hindered trade. We should work for 'free trade'. Each country would make those goods that it could produce most efficiently and trade with other countries for the rest. Goods would be cheap, increased trade would bring wealth and wages.

The most famous case of 'protectionism' was the Corn Laws passed at the end of the French Wars. The price of corn had been high during the wars as foreign corn could not be imported from Europe. Parliament, which was mostly filled with landowners, wished to keep the price high and so passed a law controlling the import of corn. The price of corn stayed high for years and caused great distress.

The manufacturers who had grown up with the Industrial Revolution were not impressed. They depended upon trade for their living. If foreign countries could not sell their goods, they had no money to buy British goods. The government began to realise this and in the 1820s duties were eased. Manufacturers opposed the Corn Laws from the beginning but in 1832 parliament was reformed and they gained more influence. The 'Anti-Corn Law League' was formed in Manchester in 1839, including MPs Richard Cobden and John Bright. The Prime Minster in the early 1840s was the son of a Lancashire mill-owner. He abolished an increasing number of customs duties, culminating in the abolition of the Corn Laws in 1846. Britain had at last carried out the 'laissez-faire' policy in which she had theoretically believed all along. Manchester still has a Free Trade Hall in memory of those days.

- ▶ Adam Smith was one of the first economists. What does an economist study?

- ▶ When did the French Wars begin and end?

- ▶ Without the revenue from customs duties the government would be in financial trouble. Which tax did Peel introduce to raise money instead?

- ▶ See if you can find out how the weather was on the side of the abolitionists.

- ▶ Who was 'Master Robert'?

'Papa Cobden taking Master Robert a Free Trade Walk' (*Punch* cartoon).

Questions

1. Draw two maps showing:-
   a. the British colonies of 1660.
   b. the British Empire of 1860.
2. Find out who each of the following was, and what he had to do with free trade:-
   William Pitt, the Younger
   William Huskisson
   Richard Cobden
   John Bright
3. How far would Adam Smith agree with Kipling's smuggler? Explain your answer.
   (If you would prefer it—you could write an imaginery conversation between the two in which each tried to explain why he was right.)
4. Explain briefly what you understand to be the meaning of 'Protection', and of 'Free Trade'.

5. In the 1660s protecting trade with the colonies was of great importance. By the 1860s, although the empire was still as important as ever, protecting trade did not matter so much. Why do you think this was? (Hint: The other chapters in this book may help with the answer.)
6. Which of the following groups of people would be 'protectionists' and which would be 'free traders'? In each case give reasons for your choice.

landowners	shopkeepers
workers	smugglers
shipowners	farmers
manufacturers	the treasury

The New Economics

Key Ideas
1. Planned economies
2. Nationalisation
3. "Never had it so good"
4. The EEC

Core Skills
1. Comprehension
2. Language
3. Research
4. Communication

Laissez-Faire

It was no part of the function of government to interfere in the economic life of the nation, indeed to interfere might well be positively harmful . . .

SOURCE 118
. . . one of the unfailing effects of increased security is a great increase of both production and of accumulation. Industry and frugality cannot exist where there is not a probability that those who labour and spare will be permitted to enjoy.
(J.S. Mill, 'Principles of Political Economy', 1847)

► Rewrite Mill's paragraph in your own words to make it more easily understandable.

The economy should be left free to react to a situation as it develops.

SOURCE 119
A rise in the profits of capital, in any trade, brings more capital to it almost instantaneously. That is to say, the free capital of a country is transmitted where it is most wanted.
(Walter Bagehot, 'Lombard Street: A Description of the Money Market', 1873)

► Bagehot feels that a rise in profits will cause more people to lend money, but profits will return to a normal level. What do you think would happen if there was a fall in the profits of capital?

Bagehot feels that if there is a high profit, more people will lend money and the profit will be spread among more lenders. Each lender will then get, not a high profit, but a normal profit. This is an example of a feeling among the Victorians that there was a system of 'checks and balances' built into the system. Things were better not interfered with, indeed to interfere might well be positively harmful.

A new approach?

This was generally accepted during the early nineteenth century when things were going well for Britain. As time went on things began to change; the Great Depression of the 1870s, the effects of the First World War, depression again in the 1930s, the effects of the Second World War. It had become increasingly clear to many people that governments would have to follow an economic policy as well as those for foreign affairs and law and order.

By the 1930s some felt the situation had become so serious that the government should become involved.

SOURCE 120
Some of our staple industries need to be refitted on modern lines, a substantial capital expenditure. In several cases there is much to be said for replanning an industry as a whole.

New capital investment at home would create additional employment. We think that a body should be set up (the Board of National Investment) in the hands of which all matters relating to schemes of long-term national investment would be concentrated.
('Minority Report of the Macmillan Committee', 1930-31)

The government did not go as far as that but they did intervene. They began to help both farmers and manufacturers. A grant was made to complete the liner Queen Mary, but in return the Cunard and White Star companies had to amalgamate. 'Special Areas' were designated and industry was encouraged to move there. Central selling arrangements were set up for coal, and the cotton industry was helped in replacing old machinery.

All of this however was done in response to individual needs. There was no overall plan nor was there an underlying philosophy. This was to be provided by a Cambridge economist J.M. Keynes. He argued that the problem stemmed from the fact that people did not sell goods. Workers who made goods were therefore thrown out of work. This meant still less money around to buy goods and the problem got worse and worse. He felt that if the government spent money helping industry to invest this would both make industry more efficient and create jobs. Those who had work would buy goods, manufacturers would have to make more, creating new jobs etc. The remedy was clear.

SOURCE 121
I conceive that a comprehensive socialisation of investment will prove the only means of securing an approximation to full employment.
(J.M. Keynes)

In using the term socialisation he is not making a party political point, but merely saying the country (or government) would have to invest. After the Second World War the government agreed.

SOURCE 122
In January 1940 the Royal Commission on the Distribution of Population reported that the best distribution of industry and population would not come about without continual guidance by the government.
(Hugh Dalton, 'The Fateful Years', 1957)

▶ Which did the government feel were the key areas of the economy in the 1940s?

SOURCE 123
Williams:
Had you a complete working pattern of policy already in mind when you became Prime Minister?

Attlee:
Certainly. Fundamental nationalisation had got to go ahead because it fell in with the planning, the essential planning of the country. It wasn't just nationalisation for nationalisation's sake, but the policy in which we believed: that fundamental things—central banking, transport, fuel and power—must be taken over by the nation.
(Attlee & Francis-Williams, 'A Prime Minister Remembers', 1961)

FORWARD!

The Prime Minister, Edward Heath, was convinced of the need to join the EEC.

▶ What do the letters EEC stand for?

▶ What is the common phrase used instead of EEC?

▶ What did Edward Heath see as the three main reasons for joining the EEC?

The policy of government involvement in the economy seemed to work and few political parties would wish to go back. Britain prospered particularly during the 1960s and the Prime Minister, Harold Macmillan, coined the slogan 'You've never had it so good'. Things were not all that they seemed however as a lot of Britain's prosperity was based on borrowing. British industry was not really earning enough to pay for all the spending. During the 1970s our way of life had to become more realistic. Other countries would only lend to us if we stopped being extravagant.

In order to sell more goods abroad to pay for our spending the quality of British goods had to improve, as did our designs. The price of British goods had to go down. We had to become more efficient. This has led to unemployment in many industries as automatic machines have been increasingly used. Once again a similar pattern to the 1930s has appeared. Areas in which the older industries are based are suffering, while areas in which new, up-to-date industries are based are prosperous.

By 1961 the British Government wished to join the EEC. It was felt that Britain was no longer rich enough to work entirely independently.

SOURCE 124

In the first place we have a strong desire to play a full part in the development of European institutions. The second consideration has been the increasing realisation that, in a world where political and economic power is being concentrated to such a great extent, a larger European unity has become essential. The third factor determining our decision has been the remarkable success of your Community and the strides which you have made towards unity in the political and economic fields.
(Edward Heath, Speech to Ministers of Member States of the EEC, 1961)

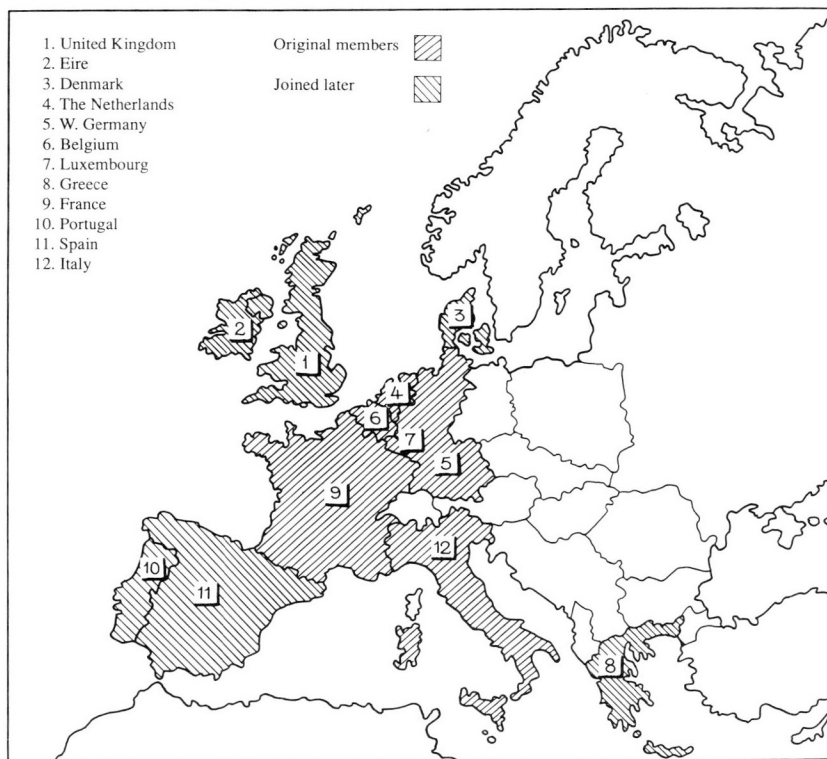

1. United Kingdom
2. Eire
3. Denmark
4. The Netherlands
5. W. Germany
6. Belgium
7. Luxembourg
8. Greece
9. France
10. Portugal
11. Spain
12. Italy

Original members
Joined later

The European Economic Community, 1989.

It took three attempts by governments of both political parties but by 1971 Britain finally joined the EEC. By 1981 the ten countries which then comprised the EEC accounted for more than one third of world trade. Some of this was because they were busy trading with each other.

Privatisation

Since 1979, when a Conservative government came to power under Margaret Thatcher, nationalisation has gone into reverse. It was felt that nationalised industries were often inefficient as they had no competition. The result was that their costs could go up and the taxpayer simply had to pay. In private industry if you do not provide what the customer wants, you go out of business. Many industries were sold off, de-nationalised, or privatised, such as British Telecom, British Gas, British Aerospace, British National Oil Corporation, British Airways, British Petroleum (BP). Others, such as British Rail lost part of their organisation, British Rail Engineering Ltd. In the 1980s there is a very real disagreement as to the extent of government control over the economy.

Questions

1. Find out the meaning of the following terms:
frugal(ity)	labour
spare	depression
capital	profit
staple	investment
amalgamate	nationalisation

2. Why was British industry in a bad state by the 1930s? (You might re-read the previous chapter to help with this.)

3. Explain clearly why some economists felt that government interference in the economy might do more harm than good.

4. A new group of economists led by Keynes felt that the country would only recover if the government was prepared to become involved. Explain his argument.

5. See if you can find out exactly what arguments have been used in favour of 'privatisation'.

6. Make a list of as many industries as you can find that were nationalised after 1920. Make a second list of those that have since been de-nationalised.

Modern Britain

Key Ideas
1. Location of Industry
2. Location of Population
3. Trade patterns
4. A divided nation

Core Skills
1. Research
2. Statistical
3. Synthesis
4. Mapwork

The problem

SOURCE 125 — Population and unemployment

	Population %			Unemployment %	
	1921	1971	1985	1975	1987
Scotland	11.1	9.4	9.1	5.3	14.0
Wales	6.0	4.9	5.0	5.8	13.5
Northern Ireland	2.9	2.8	2.8	8.0	18.4
England:					
North	6.9	5.9	5.4	6.0	15.1
North-West	13.7	12.1	11.3	5.4	13.9
Yorks & Humberside	9.3	8.6	8.6	4.1	12.4
East Midlands	5.3	6.1	6.9	3.8	10.0
West Midlands	8.0	9.2	9.2	4.4	12.4
South-West	6.2	6.8	7.8	5.0	9.3
East Anglia	2.8	3.0	3.5	3.7	8.4
South-East	28.0	31.0	30.4	3.0	8.0
United Kingdom	100	100	100	4.3	11.0

► Add up the total population in the northern areas of England in 1921 and 1971. What is the percentage change in those 50 years? What has happened in the south and east during the same period? Have any other areas declined besides the northern areas of England?

► Shade in unemployment for the different regions on a map of Britain. Use 3 colours:
   1-3%
   4-5%
   Over 5%

Britain today is a changing country. The North, which was the heart of the Industrial Revolution has been less prosperous than the South for some years, and the gap is widening. Once-great cities which were the heart of industry, such as Manchester, Glasgow, Newcastle and Birmingham are in decline. Successive governments have tried to come to terms with the problem.

Development areas

There are certain areas of the country chosen as Development Areas. Companies which set up factories in these areas are given certain incentives by the government, or the EEC. These vary from time to time.

SOURCE 126 — Incentive from the government, 1976
22% grants on all capital projects (building etc)
cheap loans
up to 80% removal grants
interest relief
training grants up to £600 if worker moved into Development Area
free fares, lodgings allowances for workers moved into Development Areas
£2 to company for every adult employed
factories available for sale or rent—up to 5 years rent-free
no planning permission needed to build
government contracts more likely to be given to companies in Development Areas
EEC gives loans on favourable terms

Britain in the 1980s.

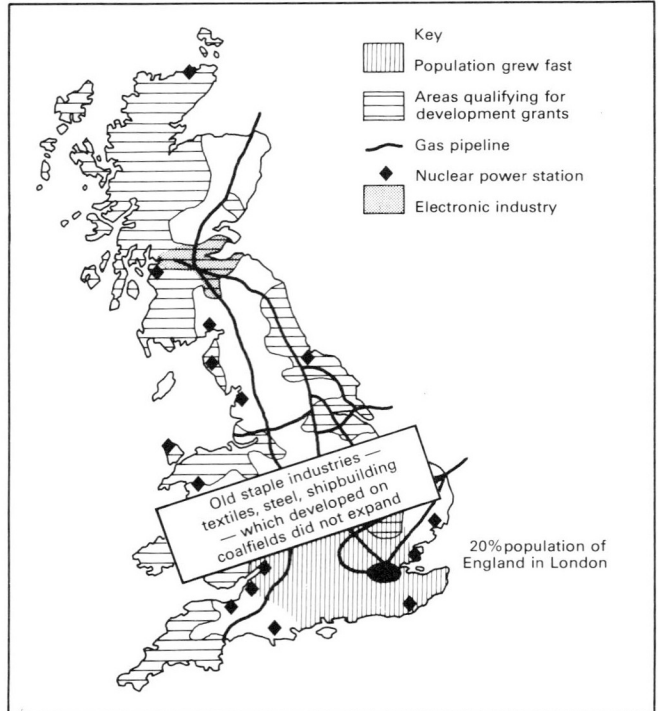

Key
- [vertical lines] Population grew fast
- [horizontal lines] Areas qualifying for development grants
- [line] Gas pipeline
- ◆ Nuclear power station
- [shaded] Electronic industry

Old staple industries — textiles, steel, shipbuilding — which developed on coalfields did not expand

20% population of England in London

The Conservative government which came into power in 1979 believes that competition is good in the longer term. Even if it may cause difficulties at a particular time, in the longer term it forces industries to be more efficient, to keep prices down, to use the best designs. One result of that is that the number of development areas has been reduced, but incentives are still used to encourage industry to develop in under-used areas.

The situation is not all bad. If the North and West are suffering high unemployment and a declining population, the South and East are not. If manufacturing industry is declining, service industries are growing. The South East is booming. Many industries are moving to small towns and rural areas. Living standards of those in work are still rising, though only slowly in many parts of the country.

Industry

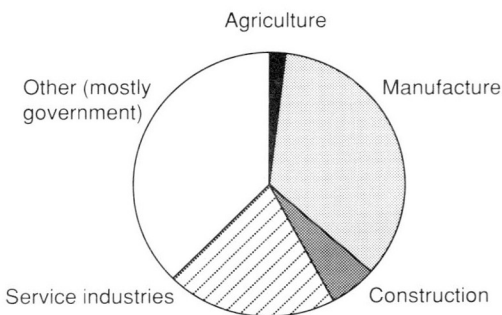

Agriculture
Other (mostly government)
Manufacture
Service industries
Construction

National Income 1985

Declining

Agriculture
Coal
Shipbuilding & Marine
  Engineering
Textiles
Transport & Communications
Distributive Trades
Fishing

Expanding

Engineering
Electrical Goods
Financial, Business,
  Professional & Scientific
  Services
Miscellaneous Services
Motor Vehicles

► What kinds of industry are
  a. growing?
  b. declining?

Change in employment (% employed) 1921 and 1987

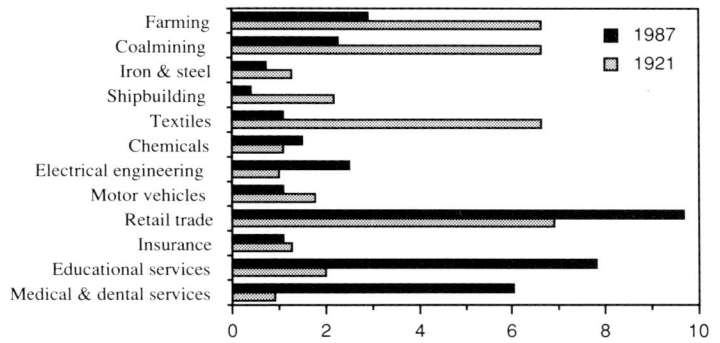

Growth

Electronics in particular is expanding quickly, especially in the central valley of Scotland between Edinburgh and Glasgow, known as 'Silicon Glen', and in the area round Cambridge.

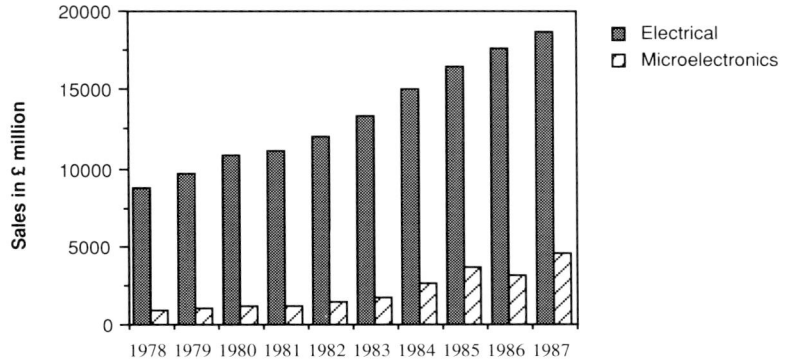

Sales of UK manufactured goods 1978-1987

Britain was helped by a happy coincidence. Oil was discovered in the North Sea in 1969. In 1975 the oil began to flow, reaching a peak of production in 1986. Towards the end of the 1970s world trade began to slow down. Some British industries were badly affected, but the economy as a whole was cushioned from the worst effects by oil from the North Sea. Oil, although perhaps past its peak, still has a lot to offer Britain.

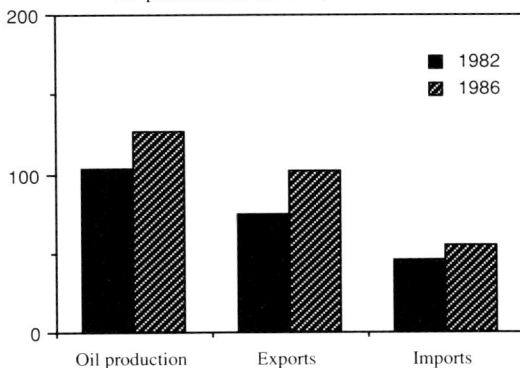

Oil produced in the UK (million tonnes)

An oil rig.

97

Consumer Expenditure

	1953	1987
	(percentage)	
Food	30.5	19.6
Fuel & Light	4.0	5.9
Durable goods	6.2	7.8
Running costs of vehicles	1.5	6.9
Holidays abroad	1.4	6.0

▶ The percentage consumer expenditure on food went down between 1953 and 1973. Does this mean that we are eating less? Explain your answer.

In spite of the problems, life for the majority is better than it has ever been before. People can sit at home and receive entertainment from the other end of the earth. They can travel for a holiday in another country effortlessly, and at speeds our ancestors did not even dream of. Even work, hard as it may be, is easier for most people than could ever have been imagined. Machines make light of jobs which would have been impossible at one time.

SOURCE 127
Change is not made without inconvenience, even from worse to better.
(Richard Hooker, 1554?-1600)

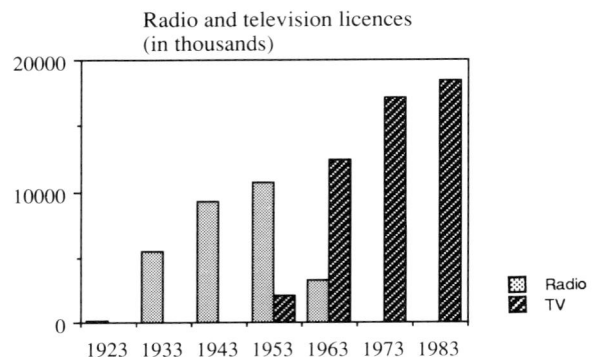

Radio and television licences (in thousands)

Questions

1. Choose key words from the following list which seem to you to be relevent to Britain today:
   technology
   unemployment
   rich
   rural
   influential
   declining
   hopeful
   changing
   backward
2. Apart from electricity and oil there is one other source of power used in the 19th and 20th centuries. What was it? Where did it come from before 1970? After 1970?
3. Find out the meaning of primary, secondary and tertiary production. Using these terms what has happened to British industry since the Second World War?
4. Mark in the regions of Britain on a blank map. Shade the regions in different colours according to the following population change:
   Fallen over 1%
   Fallen 0-1%
   Grown 0-1%
   Grown 1-2%
   Grown over 2%
   Compare the result with the map you shaded in for the side question on page 95. Comment on the comparison.
5. Use an atlas to sort out where the major British oilfields are situated. Which towns are likely to benefit from the work involved in supplying the oil rigs? Are these in areas of high unemployment or low unemployment? What will happen when the oil runs out?
6. Outline the changes in British industry during the 20th century.

Relative value of the £ (1850 = £1)

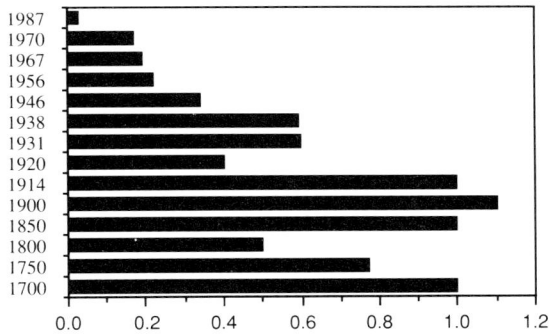

Balance of payments 1855-1987

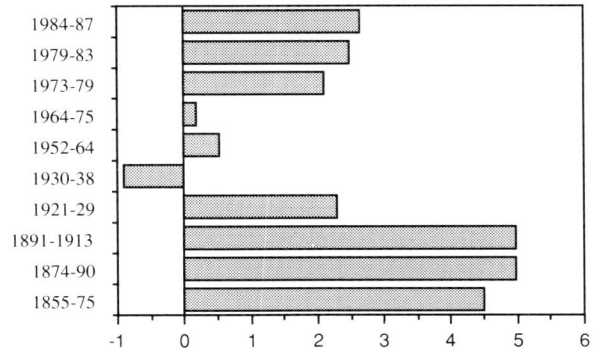

Old and new

Money

Old Money	Written	or	New Money
Guinea	£1 1s 0d		£1.05
Pound	£1 0s 0d	£1	£1
Crown (5 shillings or 5 bob)	5s	5/-	25p
Half-a-crown	2s 6d	2/6	12$\frac{1}{2}$p
Florin (2 shillings or 2 bob)	2s 0d	2/-	10p
Shilling	1s 0d	1/-	5p
Sixpence (a tanner)	6d		2$\frac{1}{2}$p
Halfpenny (pronounced ha'p'ney)	$\frac{1}{2}$d		
Farthing	$\frac{1}{4}$d		

Length

Old Length	Equals	New Length
1 Mile	1760 yards	1.60 km
1 Furlong	220 yards	201.1m
1 Chain	22 yards	20.1 m
1 Pole or perch	5$\frac{1}{2}$ yards	5.02 m
1 Yard	3 feet	0.91 m
1 Foot	12 inches	0.3 m
1 Inch		25.39 mm

Capacity

Old Measure	Equals	New Measure
1 Quarter	8 bushels	2.9 hectolitres
1 Bushel	8 gallons	3.5 decalitres
1 Peck	2 gallons	9.06 litres
1 Gallon	4 quarts or 8 pints	4.5 litres
1 Quart	2 pints	1.1 litres
1 Pint	4 gills or 20 fluid ounces	0.56 litres

Conversion Tables

Area

Old area	Equals	New Area
1 Square Mile	640 acres	258.9 hectares
1 Acre	4840 square yards	0.4 hectares
1 Rod	1 square pole	25.29 square metres
1 Square Yard	9 square feet	0.8 square metres
1 Square Foot	144 square inches	9.29 square decimetres
1 Square Inch		6.45 square cm

Weight

Old Weight	Equals	New Weight
1 Ton	20 cwt	1.016 tonnes
1 Hundredweight (1 cwt)	112 lbs	50.8 kg
1 Quarter	28 lbs	12.7 kg
1 Stone	14 lbs	6.35 kg
1 Pound (1 lb)	16 oz	0.15 kg
1 oz (1 ounce)		28.34 grams

Glossary

Bloomery	early type of small furnace for smelting iron; usually with hand-worked bellows
Blower	an escape of gas (in a coal mine)
Calamity	disaster
Carding	combing the fibres straight (like combing your hair)
Celerity	quickness
Census	count of the population
Chauldron	an old measure of coal used in the North East of England; a Newcastle chauldron was equal to 53cwt (2692.4kg)
Chronology	to do with time, dates
Clipper	type of fast sailing ship
Contrivance	mechanical device
Entrepreneur	businessman who owns, or controls, a business
Erection	building
Flamboyant	highly decorated, showy
Finishing	those processes carried out on cloth after it has been woven, eg bleaching, dyeing
Gin	strictly an 'engine' or machine, but normally used in earlier days to mean a hand-driven windlass to wind things up and down a well, or mine.
Glaze	a liquid in which a pot is dipped to make it glossy usually then fired in a kiln
Hydraulic	driven by water-power
Hydraulic engine	engine or machine worked by water (today any fluid)
Imprimis	first
Incentive	encouragement to do something
Jasper ware	plain, unglazed pottery (usually blue, green or black) with raised figures from Greek or Roman mythology in white
Languor	faintness, tiredness

Loam	paste of clay and water
Manufactory	factory
Mensuration	measuring
Metallurgy	art and science applied to metals, and their study
op. cit.	book (work) previously mentioned
Portents	signs of what is to come
Predicament	unpleasant or difficult situation
Protectionism	putting customs duties (taxes) on imported foreign goods to make them more expensive to buy than your own home-produced goods
Prowess	bravery or gallantry
P.s.i.	pounds per square inch (1 p.s.i. = $0.0703 kg/cm^2$)
Quartern	loaf of 4 pounds (lbs) weight
Sagacity	wisdom
Sediment	grains of heavy material that settle to the bottom of a liquid
Synthesis	combining together different pieces of information
Warp	threads stretched along the loom to be woven in and out by the weft
Weft	threads stretched across the loom, weaving in and out of the warp
Woodlump	stack of wood

Index